Baby & Me Knits

Baby & Me Knits

20 timeless knitted designs for baby & mom

Celeste Young

SELLERS
PUBLISHING

Published by **Sellers Publishing, Inc**.
161 John Roberts Road, South Portland, Maine 04106

Visit our Web site: www.sellerspublishing.com
E-mail:rsp@rsvp.com

Design and layout copyright © 2015 BlueRed Press
Text Copyright © 2015 Celeste Young
Patterns and templates copyright © Celeste Young
Cover photography © Ashley Eipp
Photography by John Ostrander IV and Celeste Young
All rights reserved
Design by Cara Rogers

ISBN 13: 978-1-4162-4541-4

Library of Congress Number: 2014945268

10 9 8 7 6 5 4 3 2 1

Printed and Bound in China

Contents

* Knits for Mom

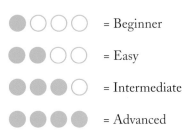

Difficulty Key

●○○○ = Beginner

●●○○ = Easy

●●●○ = Intermediate

●●●● = Advanced

Knitting Needle Sizes	
METRIC SIZES(mm)	US SIZES
2.0	0
2.25	1
2.75	2
3.0	–
3.25	3
3.5	4
3.75	5
4.0	6
4.5	7
5.0	8
5.5	9
6.0	10
6.5	10.5
7.0	–
7.5	–
8.0	11
9.0	13
10.0	15
12.75	17
15.0	19
19.0	35
25.0	50

Introduction

Baby & Me Knits is a celebration of my two great passions: my infant son, Jack, and knitting!

I had the distinction of writing my second book and having my first baby at the same time, quite different than the experience of my first book, *Knits of a Feather* (Sellers Publishing, 2013)! Looking back, a new baby and a new book require incredible creativity, limitless patience, countless late nights, and a good dose of humility. Jack has been such a tremendous source of joy and inspiration for me and for my husband and co-photographer, John. With Jack as one of our models, Baby & Me Knits has truly been a family affair!

As a mom I know how important it is to have things that are practical, wearable, and washable for my baby and myself. My collection begins here, and aims to share the lessons I have found to be most useful in my knitting career — from casting on to finishing! These goals lead me to design items that are great for babies, parents, and knitters alike. The patterns in this book are designed to work individually and in sets, perfect for creating heirlooms for your family or special gifts for an amazing parent and child. I have left plenty of room for interpretation in my designs so that you can add your personal flair to them. Choose your own color scheme for the Sweet Berries set, for example, or knit simple or wildly striped socks and fingerless gloves from the Bright Stripe set, or increase your yarn gauge and repeat count on any of the baby blankets to create a full-sized throw. It is my hope that *Baby & Me Knits* will introduce you to fun, new techniques and empower you to be creative as you make these sweet knitted pieces. Please write to me on my website at celesteyoungdesigns.com, or post photos on my facebook page or ravelry group. I can't wait to hear about your results!

Celeste Young

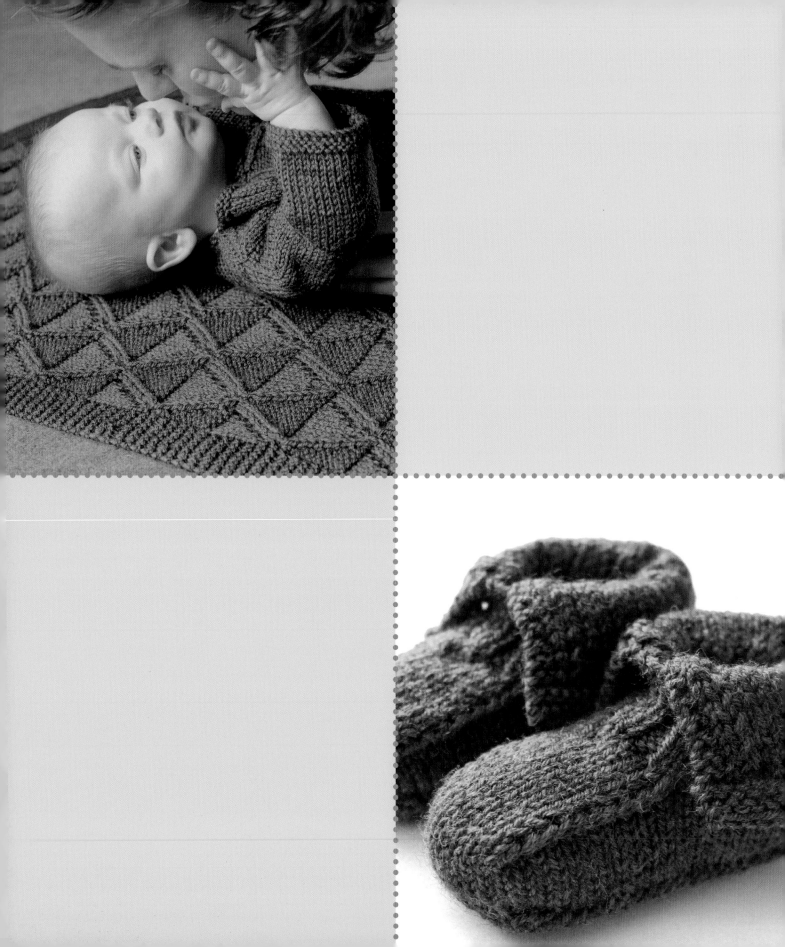

Baby Kale

Blanket

Booties

Shawl

Boatneck

Baby Kale Blanket

This blanket features a bold, all over lace pattern that shines in a rich shade of green. Create an heirloom gift for a special baby, sure to comfort and last in a stunning superwash wool!

Difficulty Level

Finished Size
27" wide, 30" long

Yarn
Cascade 220 Superwash (100% Superwash Wool; 220 yd [200 m]/100 g): #1918 Shire, 4 skeins.

Needles
Size 8 (5 mm) 24" circular, or size needed to obtain gauge

Notions
Stitch markers; tapestry needle; scissors.

Gauge
20 stitches, 26 rows = 4" in pattern stitch (after blocking)

Glossary of Abbreviations
BO – bind off
CO – cast on
k – knit
k2tog – knit two stitches together
m – marker, markers
p – purl
pm – place marker
RS – right side
sl – slip
ssk – slip first stitch as if to knit, slip second stitch as if to knit, then insert left hand needle through the fronts of both stitches together and knit.
st, sts – stitch, stitches
WS – wrong side
yo – yarn over

Stitch Patterns
Baby Kale Blanket stitch pattern:
Row 1 (RS): (k1, yo, ssk, p11, k2tog, yo) 8 times, k1.
Row 2 (WS): p1, (p2, k11, p3) 8 times.
Row 3: (k1, yo, k1, ssk, p9, k2tog, k1, yo) 8 times, k1.
Row 4: p1, (p3, k9, p4) 8 times.
Row 5: (k2, yo, k1, ssk, p7, k2tog, k1, yo, k1) 8 times, k1.
Row 6: p1, (p4, k7, p5) 8 times.
Row 7: (k3, yo, k1, ssk, p5, k2tog, k1, yo, k2) 8 times, k1.
Row 8: p1, (p5, k5, p6) 8 times.
Row 9: (k4, yo, k1, ssk, p3, k2tog, k1, yo, k3) 8 times, k1.
Row 10: p1, (p6, k3, p7) 8 times.
Row 11: (k5, yo, k1, ssk, p1, k2tog, k1, yo, k4) 8 times, k1.
Row 12: p1, (p7, k1, p8) 8 times.
Row 13: (p6, k2tog, yo, k1, yo, ssk, p5) 8 times, p1.
Row 14: k1, (k5, p5, k6) 8 times.
Row 15: (p5, k2tog, k1, yo, k1, yo, k1, ssk, p4) 8 times, p1.
Row 16: k1, (k4, p7, k5) 8 times.
Row 17: (p4, k2tog, k1, yo, k3, yo, k1, ssk, p3) 8 times, p1.
Row 18: k1, (k3, p9, k4) 8 times.
Row 19: (p3, k2tog, k1, yo, k5, yo, k1, ssk, p2) 8 times, p1.
Row 20: k1, (k2, p11, k3) 8 times.
Row 21: (p2, k2tog, k1, yo, k7, yo, k1, ssk, p1) 8 times, p1.
Row 22: k1 (k1, p13, k2) 8 times.
Row 23: (p1, k2tog, k1, yo, k9, yo, k1, ssk) 8 times, p1.
Row 24: k1, (p15, k1) 8 times.

Pattern
Using cable method, CO 129 sts.
Slipping the first stitch of each row as if to knit, k 16 rows. Continue slipping first stitch of each row throughout blanket.
Next row (RS): K8 for right border, pm, begin Baby Kale pattern, reading chart from right to left on all right side rows: work sts 1–16 8 times, work st 17, pm, k8 for left border.
Next row (WS): K8 border sts, sl m, reading chart from left to right on all wrong side rows, work st 17, work sts 16–1 8 times, sl m, k8 border sts.
Continue in pattern as established, repeating chart rows 1–24 a total of 9 times.
K 16 rows. BO all sts knitwise.
Weave in ends and block to finished measurements.

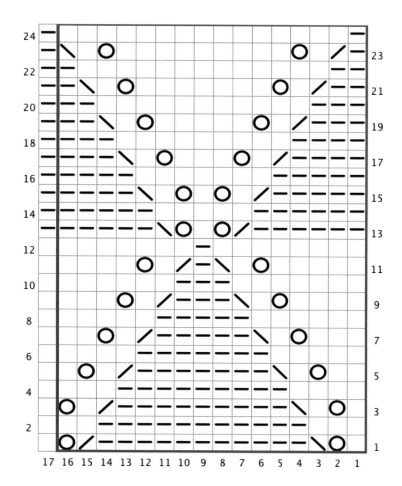

KEY

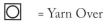 = Knit
(RS) Knit
(WS) Purl

⟋ = Knit 2 together

— = Purl
(RS) Purl
(WS) Knit

⟍ = Slip slip knit

◯ = Yarn Over

YARN OVER INCREASE

1: Knit to the location of the planned yarn over.

2: Bring the working yarn to the front of the work, between the needles.

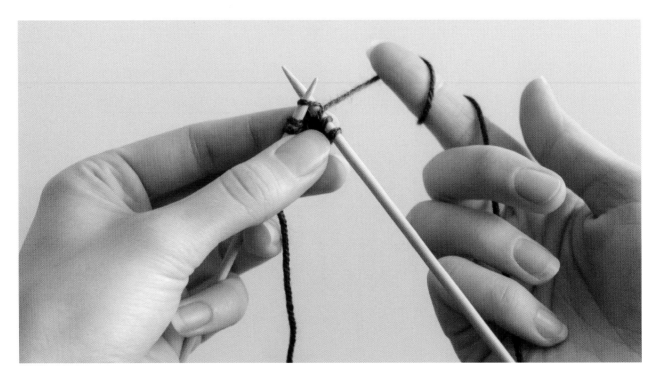

3: Insert the right hand needle into the next stitch to be worked, and as you prepare to knit, the working yarn will wrap over and around the right hand needle.

4: Finish knitting the stitch, and the yarn over will also be created. Note that yarn over stitch is the second stitch from the tip of the right hand needle, and appears to be leaning to the left.

Difficulty Level

Finished Size
3–6 (6–12, 18–24) months

Yarn
Cascade 220 Superwash (100% Superwash Wool; 220 yd [200 m]/100 g): #1918 Shire, 1 skein.

Needles
Size 5 (3.75 mm) set of 5 double-pointed

Notions
Stitch marker; tapestry needle; scissors.

Gauge
23 stitches, 22 ridges (44 rows) = 4" in garter stitch

Glossary of Abbreviations
BO – bind off
CO – cast on
k – knit
k2tog – knit two stitches together
m – marker
p – purl
p2tog – purl two stitches together
pm – place marker
rem – remain
rep – repeat
RS – right side
sl – slip stitch as if to purl
ssk – slip first stitch as if to knit, slip second stitch as if to knit, then insert left hand needle through the fronts of both stitches together and knit.
st, sts – stitch, stitches
WS – wrong side
yo – yarn over

Baby Kale Booties

These sweet booties are knit to fit a range of baby feet, and feature ribbed cuffs to keep them nice and snug! The foldover cuff adds a whimsical touch, while the one-piece design makes them the perfect last-minute project!

Stitch Patterns
Stockinette stitch (in the round)
Round 1 and all following rounds: knit.
k2, p2 rib (in the round)
Round 1 and all following rounds: (k2, p2) around.

Pattern
Beginning at sole and using cable method, CO 8 (10, 12) sts.
Beginning on the RS, k 32 (40, 48) rows (16 [20, 24] ridges) in garter st, ending on a WS row.
Next row (RS): K 8 (10, 12) sts, do not turn. Instead, rotate work (RS still facing) 90° clockwise. Using empty needle, pick up 1 st in each ridge along long side (16 [20, 24] sts picked up). Rotate work 90° clockwise again, and using another empty needle, pick up 1 st in each st along short side (8 [10, 12] sts picked up). Rotate work 90° clockwise for final time, and using another empty needle, pick up 1 st in each st along long side (16 [20, 24] sts picked up; total of 48 [60, 72] sts around sole). Do not turn. Pm and join to begin knitting in the round. Work even in st st until work measures 1.5" from picked up edge.
Begin working back and forth in short rows for top of bootie: K7 [9, 11] ssk,

turn work.
Next row (WS): Sl1, p6 [8, 10] p2tog, turn work.
Next row (RS): Sl1, k6 [8, 10] ssk, turn work.
Repeat last two rows 6 [8, 10] times more, then work one more WS row as established (32 [40, 48] sts rem).
With RS facing, join and pm to resume working in the round.
Work in (k2, p2) rib for 1.5 (1.75, 2)". Back of bootie measured from sole is 3 (3.25, 3.5)" high.
Resume working back and forth in rows for foldover cuff, beginning with RS facing: remove m, work 4 (5, 6) sts in ribbing pattern to center of cuff over toe of bootie. Replace m to indicate beginning/end of row until work is established.
Turn work to WS of bootie (will be RS of foldover cuff when turned down) and k3, ssk, yo, k until 5 sts rem before m, yo, k2tog, k3.
Turn work to RS of bootie (will be WS of foldover cuff when turned down) and k2, p until 2 sts rem, k2.
Rep last two rows 5 times more, ending on a purl row. K4 rows and BO all sts knitwise. Weave in ends, turn down cuff, and block lightly.

PICKING UP STITCHES AROUND BOOTIE SOLE

1: At the end of the row, do not turn work. Instead, rotate work 90⁰ clockwise with RS facing.

2: Using empty needle, insert tip into the first garter ridge bump along the edge, yo, and draw up a new stitch.

3: Continue to pick up new stitches, one in each garter ridge bump along the edge.

4: Upon completion of each side, slide the newly picked up stitches to the center of the needle before progressing to the next side. Use a new needle for each side.

Difficulty Level

Finished Size
Shawlette: 41" wide, 19" deep (Shawl: 53" wide, 24.75" deep)
Shown in shawlette size.

Yarn
Cascade 220 Superwash (100% Superwash Wool; 220 yd [200 m]/100 g): #1918 Shire, 2 (3) skeins.

Needles
Size 8 (5 mm) 24" circular, or size needed to obtain gauge

Notions
Stitch markers; tapestry needle; scissors.

Gauge
17 stitches, 26 rows = 4" in stockinette stitch (after blocking)

Glossary of Abbreviations
BO – bind off
CO – cast on
k – knit
k2tog – knit two stitches together
m – marker, markers
p – purl
pm – place marker
rep – repeat
RS – right side
sl – slip
ssk – slip first stitch as if to knit, slip second stitch as if to knit, then insert left hand needle through the fronts of both stitches together and knit.
st, sts – stitch, stitches
WS – wrong side
yo – yarn over

Baby Kale Shawl

Perfect for layering on a cool day, wrapping up baby, or using as a nursing cover, this shawl is sure to come in handy for any mom! Knit one for yourself or as a sweet, thoughtful gift for an expectant mother. The stockinette body is quick to knit while the lace patterned edge provides a touch of elegance.

Stitch Patterns
Baby Kale Shawl Edging Chart
Row 1 (RS): (k1, yo, ssk, p11, k2tog, yo) 5 (7) times, k1.
Row 2 (WS): p1, (p2, k11, p3) 5 (7) times.
Row 3: yo, (k1, yo, k1, ssk, p9, k2tog, k1, yo) 5 (7) times, k1, yo.
Row 4: p2, (p3, k9, p4) 5 (7) times, p1.
Row 5: yo, k1, (k2, yo, k1, ssk, p7, k2tog, k1, yo, k1) 5 (7) times, k2, yo.
Row 6: p3, (p4, k7, p5) 5 (7) times, p2.
Row 7: yo, k2, (k3, yo, k1, ssk, p5, k2tog, k1, yo, k2) 5 (7) times, k3, yo.
Row 8: p4, (p5, k5, p6) 5 (7) times, p3.
Row 9: yo, k3, (k4, yo, k1, ssk, p3, k2tog, k1, yo, k3) 5 (7) times, k4, yo.
Row 10: p5, (p6, k3, p7) 5 (7) times, p4.
Row 11: yo, k4, (k5, yo, k1, ssk, p1, k2tog, k1, yo, k4) 5 (7) times, k5, yo.
Row 12: p6, (p7, k1, p8) 5 (7) times, p5.
Row 13: yo, p5, (p6, k2tog, yo, k1, yo, ssk, p5) 5 (7) times, p6, yo.
Row 14: p1, k6, (k5, p5, k6) 5 (7) times, k5, p1.
Row 15: yo, k2, p4, (p5, k2tog, k1, yo, k1, yo, k1, ssk, p4) 5 (7) times, p5, k2, yo.
Row 16: p3, k5, (k4, p7, k5) 5 (7) times, k4, p3.
Row 17: yo, k1, yo, k1, ssk, p3, (p4, k2tog, k1, yo, k3, yo, k1, ssk, p3) 5 (7) times, p4, k2tog, k1, yo, k1, yo.

Row 18: p5, k4, (k3, p9, k4) 5 (7) times, k3, p5.
Row 19: yo, k3, yo, k1, ssk, p2, (p3, k2tog, k1, yo, k5, yo, k1, ssk, p2) 5 (7) times, p3, k2tog, k1, yo, k3, yo.
Row 20: p7, k3, (k2, p11, k3) 5 (7) times, k2, p7.
Row 21: yo, k5, yo, k1, ssk, p1, (p2, k2tog, k1, yo, k7, yo, k1, ssk, p1) 5 (7) times, p2, k2tog, k1, yo, k5, yo.
Row 22: p9, k2, (k1, p13, k2) 5 (7) times, k1, p9.
Row 23: yo, k7, yo, k1, ssk, (p1, k2tog, k1, yo, k9, yo, k1, ssk) 5 (7) times, p1, k2tog, k1, yo, k7, yo.
Row 24: p11, k1, (p15, k1) 5 (7) times, p11.

Pattern
Using cable method, CO 5 sts.
Row 1: (RS): k2, yo, k1, yo, k2 (7 sts).
Row 2: (WS): knit.
Row 3: k2, pm, yo, k1, yo, pm, k1, pm, yo, k1, yo, pm, k2 (11 sts).
Row 4: Slipping all markers as you come to them, k2, p to last 2 sts, k2.
Row 5: k2, sl m, yo, k to next m, yo, sl m, k1 (center stitch), sl m, yo, k to last m, yo, k2.
Rep last two rows until there are 167 (231) sts, ending on a WS row.

Work Baby Kale Shawl Edging

Row 1 (RS): Reading from right to left, k2, sl m, work chart repeat 5 (7) times, work chart to m, sl m, k1 (center stitch), sl m, work chart repeat 5 (7) times, work chart to m, sl m, k2.

Row 2 (WS): Reading from left to right, k2, sl m, work chart to repeat, work chart repeat 5 (7) times, work chart to m, sl m, p1, sl m, work chart to repeat, work chart repeat 5 (7) times, sl m, k2.

Continue working as established until chart is completed, ending on a WS row. Knit 4 rows, then BO knitwise.

Finishing

Weave in all ends. Soak shawl in tepid water, then block and pin to finished measurements.

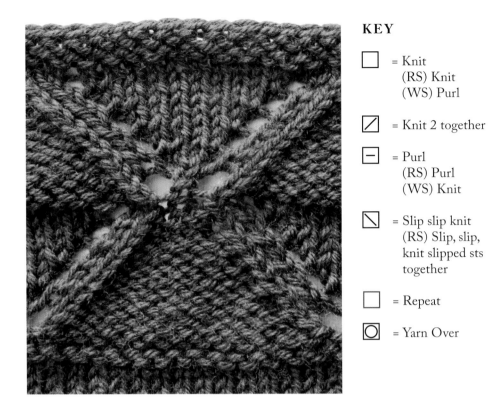

KEY

☐ = Knit
(RS) Knit
(WS) Purl

▱ = Knit 2 together

− = Purl
(RS) Purl
(WS) Knit

◲ = Slip slip knit
(RS) Slip, slip,
knit slipped sts
together

☐ = Repeat

⊙ = Yarn Over

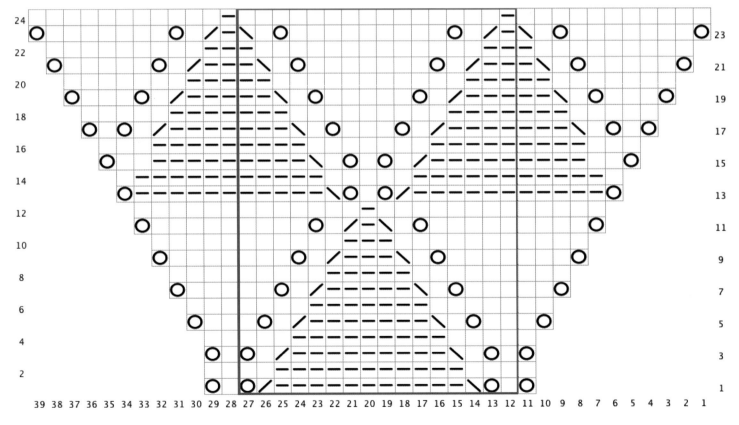

CABLE CAST ON

1: Begin with a slip knot, place on left hand needle as first stitch, then insert right hand needle as if to knit.

2: Yarn over and draw through a new loop of yarn, gently stretching new loop out and keeping slip knot (first stitch) on the left hand needle.

3: Transfer new loop onto left hand needle as next stitch, slipping from tip to tip without twisting.

4: For next and all following stitches, insert right hand needle into space between the newest stitch and the previous stitch. Photo shows correct needle placement, revealing both legs of newest stitch when right needle is placed between stitches and needles are tipped towards the knitter for better visibility.

Difficulty Level

Finished Size
3 (6, 12, 18, 24) months. Shown in size 6 months, modeled on an 18 pound baby.

Yarn
Cascade 220 Superwash (100% Superwash Wool; 220 yd [200 m]/100 g): #1918 Shire, 1 (2, 2, 2, 2) skeins.

Needles
Size 7 (4.5 mm) straight, or size needed to obtain gauge

Notions
Stitch markers; tapestry needle; scissors.

Gauge
20 stitches, 28 rows = 4" in stockinette stitch

Glossary of Abbreviations
BO – bind off
CO – cast on
k – knit
k2tog – knit two stitches together to decrease
LL – Left leaning lifted increase: Using left hand needle, lift the stitch below the stitch you just knit on the right hand needle from the back and knit it.
LR – Right leaning lifted increase: Using right hand needle, lift the stitch below the stitch on the left hand needle from the back and knit it.
m – marker, markers
p – purl
pm – place marker
rep – repeat
RS – right side
sl m – slip marker
ssk – slip two stitches individually as if to knit, then insert left hand needle into the front of those slipped stitches and knit them together to decrease.
st st – stockinette stitch
st, sts – stitch, stitches
WS – wrong side
yo – yarn over

Baby Kale Boatneck

Knit in soft superwash wool, this sweater is cozy to wear and easy to care for. The central lace panel adds just a touch of peek-a-boo fun for curious fingers – layer with a bright color to make a fashion statement!

Stitch Patterns
Stockinette Stitch
Row 1 (RS): knit.
Row 2 (WS): purl.
Rep rows 1 and 2 for length stated.
Baby Kale Boatneck stitch pattern:
Row 1 (RS): k1, yo, ssk, p11, k2tog, yo, k1
Row 2 (WS): p3, k11, p3
Row 3: k1, yo, k1, ssk, p9, k2tog, k1, yo, k1
Row 4: p4, k9, p4
Row 5: k2, yo, k1, ssk, p7, k2tog, k1, yo, k2
Row 6: p5, k7, p5
Row 7: k3, yo, k1, ssk, p5, k2tog, k1, yo, k3
Row 8: p6, k5, p6
Row 9: k4, yo, k1, ssk, p3, k2tog, k1, yo, k4
Row 10: p7, k3, p7
Row 11: k5, yo, k1, ssk, p1, k2tog, k1, yo, k5
Row 12: p8, k1, p8
Row 13: p6, k2tog, yo, k1, yo, ssk, p6
Row 14: k6, p5, k6
Row 15: p5, k2tog, k1, yo, k1, yo, k1, ssk, p5
Row 16: k5, p7, k5
Row 17: p4, k2tog, k1, yo, k3, yo, k1, ssk, p4
Row 18: k4, p9, k4
Row 19: p3, k2tog, k1, yo, k5, yo, k1, ssk, p3
Row 20: k3, p11, k3

Row 21: p2, k2tog, k1, yo, k7, yo, k1, ssk, p2
Row 22: k2, p13, k2
Row 23: p1, k2tog, k1, yo, k9, yo, k1, ssk, p1
Row 24: k1, p15, k1

Pattern
Front
Using cable method, CO 49 (51, 57, 59, 67) sts. K4 rows.
Next row (RS): k15 (16, 19, 20, 24) sts, p1, pm, begin Baby Kale pattern, reading chart from right to left on all right side rows, pm, p1, k15 (16, 19, 20, 24) sts.
Next row (WS): p15 (16, 19, 20, 24) sts, k1, sl m, work next row of Baby Kale pattern, reading chart from left to right on all wrong side rows, sl m, k1, p15 (16, 19, 20, 24) sts.
Continue in this manner, repeating rows 1–24 until work measures 9 (10, 10.5, 11, 11.5)" long, ending on a WS.
K4 rows and BO knitwise.

Back
Using cable method, CO 52 (54, 57, 60, 67) sts. K4 rows.
Work even in st st until piece measures 9 (10, 10.5, 11, 11.5)" long or same as front, ending on a WS.
K4 rows and BO knitwise.

Sleeves (Make 2)
Using cable method, CO 32 (36, 40, 42,

44) sts. K 4 rows.

Beginning with a RS knit row, work 2 rows in st st.

Begin increasing (RS): k1, LR, k until 1 st rem, LL in stitch just worked, k1.

Beginning with a WS purl row, work 5 rows even in st st.

Work increase row. Rep these 6 rows 4 (5, 6, 7, 8) times more for a total of 42 (48, 54, 58, 62) sts.

Work even in st st until sleeve measures 6 (6.5, 7.5, 8, 8.5)" from cast-on edge, ending with a WS row. BO all sts knitwise.

Finishing

Block all sweater pieces flat. Using tapestry needle, seam front to back at shoulders, leaving center 7 (7, 7.5, 8, 8.5)" open for head and neck. Open front and back and lay sweater body flat with RS facing up, then seam each sleeve in place. Fold sweater front and back together with WS together, then join side seams and sleeve seams. Weave in all ends and re-block as necessary.

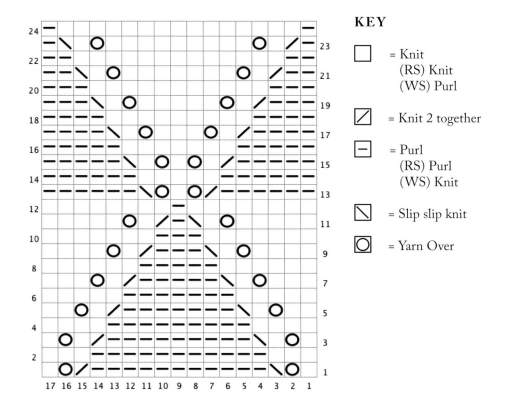

KEY

☐ = Knit
(RS) Knit
(WS) Purl

╱ = Knit 2 together

── = Purl
(RS) Purl
(WS) Knit

╲ = Slip slip knit

⊙ = Yarn Over

USING MATTRESS STITCH TO SEAM SHOULDERS
(LEFT SHOULDER SHOWN)

1: Seaming from the armhole edge in towards the neck, thread tapestry needle with seaming yarn. Working on the piece closest to you, insert needle under the two legs of the stitch just beneath the bind off edge, noting that the legs should point at the edge.

2: Draw needle through and move to the piece further from you, again inserting needle under the two legs of the stitch just beneath the bind off edge, noting that the legs should point at that edge.

3: Continue seaming in this fashion, moving from the front piece to the back piece and working one stitch at a time. Do not tighten until you have completed a few passes and can see that the two halves are aligning well.

4: Gently tighten the seaming yarn so that the two halves are cinched together.

Bright Stripe

Blanket

Cardigan

Fingerless Gloves

Baby Socks

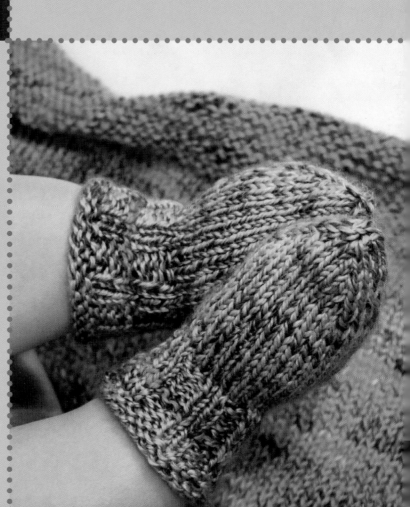

Finished Size
29" wide, 33" long

Yarn
Cascade Bentley (75% Acrylic, 25% Superwash Wool; 207 yd [200 m]/100 g): #02 Tangerine (MC), 4 skeins; #11 Lime (CC), 1 skein.

Needles
Size 7 (4.5 mm) 24" circular or size needed to obtain gauge

Notions
Stitch markers; tapestry needle; scissors.

Gauge
20 stitches, 26 rows = 4" in stockinette stitch

Glossary of Abbreviations
CC – contrast color
CO – cast on
k – knit
m – marker, markers
MC – main color
p – purl
pm – place marker
rem – remain
rep – repeat
RS – right side
sl – slip
st, sts – stitch, stitches
WS – wrong side

Bright Stripe Blanket

Simple to knit and washable too, this bright and bold blanket is just perfect in a fun, rainbow tweed yarn! Mom will love to comfort baby with this soft blanket, and baby will love to look at the bright colors!

Pattern
Using MC and cable method, CO 140 sts. Do not join; instead, work back and forth in rows on circular needles.
Beginning with a RS row, work 20 rows in garter stitch (10 ridges).
Next row (RS): k10 for right border, pm, k until 10 sts rem, pm, k10 for left border. Maintain garter stitch borders throughout blanket.
WS: k10, sl m, p to next m, sl m, k10.
Rep last two rows 2 times more, then cut MC.

Join CC and continue in pattern as established for 6 rows, working garter stitch on left and right borders and stockinette stitch in the center.
Cut CC, join MC, and work even until blanket measures 29" from CO edge.
Cut MC, join CC, and work 6 rows even (repeating stripe as previous).
Cut CC, join MC, and work even for 6 rows, removing markers on last WS row. Work 20 rows in garter stitch and bind off.

ENDING THE BIND OFF NEATLY

1: Bind off until one stitch remains on the left hand needle.

2: Using the right hand needle, lift up the stitch one row below the remaining stitch.

3: Place the lifted stitch up on the left hand needle. Knit the two stitches on the left hand needle together, then lift the stitch on the right hand needle over and off as usual.

4: Cut yarn and stretch out remaining stitch until the tail pops through. The resulting corner should lie flatter and appear much neater!

Difficulty Level

Finished Size
3 (6, 12, 18, 24) months. Shown in size 3 months, modeled on a 14 pound baby.

Yarn
Cascade Bentley (75% Acrylic, 25% Superwash Wool; 207 yd [200 m]/100 g): #02 Tangerine (MC), 1 (2, 2, 2, 2) skeins; #11 Lime (CC), 1 skein.

Needles
Size 7 (4.5 mm) 24" circular and set of 4 double-pointed; size 5 (3.75 mm) 24" circular and set of 4 double-pointed or sizes needed to obtain gauge

Notions
Stitch markers, stitch holders or scrap yarn; tapestry needle; scissors.

Gauge
21 stitches, 26 rows = 4" in stockinette stitch on larger needles

Glossary of Abbreviations
BO – bind off
CO – cast on
k – knit
k2tog – knit two stitches together to decrease
kfb – knit in the front and back of the next stitch to increase
m – marker, markers
p – purl
pm – place marker
rem – remain
rep – repeat
RS – right side
sl m – slip marker
ssk – slip two stitches individually as if to knit, then insert left hand needle into the front of those slipped stitches and knit them together to decrease.
st, sts – stitch, stitches
WS – wrong side
yo – yarn over

Bright Stripe Cardigan

Bright and bold basics are perfect for mixing and matching – like this fun, rainbow tweed yarn, set off with contrasting stripes and buttons! Mom and baby are sure to smile at this cozy, cheerful cardigan, just right for crisp fall days or summer air conditioning!

Notes
Sweater body and sleeves are worked back and forth in rows from the neck down, then sleeve stitches are placed on holders to complete the body of the sweater. You will then return to the sleeve stitches and use double-pointed needles to work them seamlessly in the round.

Pattern
Sweater yoke and body
Beginning at the neck edge with MC, smaller circular needles, and cable cast-on method, CO 60 (62, 66, 66, 68) sts. Do not join.
Rows 1–4: Knit.
Row 5 (RS): Buttonhole row, boys: k1, k2tog, yo, k to end.
Row 5 (RS): Buttonhole row, girls: K until 3 sts remain, yo, k2tog, k1.
Repeat buttonhole row for boys or girls every 20 rows (10 ridges visible in button band since last buttonhole) throughout.
Row 6: Knit.
Row 7: Change to larger circular needles and k4, pm, k9 (10, 10, 10, 11), kfb, pm, kfb, k2, kfb, pm, kfb, k22 (22, 24, 24, 24), kfb, pm, kfb, k2, kfb, pm, kfb, k9 (10, 10,

10, 11), pm, k4.
Row 8 and all WS rows: K4, p to last m, k4.
Row 9: K4, sl m, *k to 1 st before next m, kfb, sl m, kfb, rep from * three times, k to end.
Rep rows 8 and 9 until there are 164 (174, 186, 194, 204) sts total, ending after a WS row.
Next row (RS): Divide for sleeves: K4, sl m, k to next m, remove m and slip 30 (33, 35, 37, 39) sleeve sts to stitch holder or scrap yarn, remove m, k across back sts, remove m, slip 30 (33, 35, 37, 39) sleeve sts to stitch holder or scrap yarn, remove m, k to last m, sl m, k to end (104 [110, 116, 120, 126] body sts).
WS: K4, sl m, p to last m, sl m, k4.
RS: Knit.
Rep last two rows until sweater measures 7.5 (8, 8.5, 9, 9.5)" from cast on edge, ending with a WS row. Take care to lay the sweater flat and measure from the center back neck edge down without stretching the fabric or including sts on needles in your measurement.
Next row (RS): Do not cut MC; instead, leave it hanging at the edge of the buttonband. Join CC and k all sts.

Next row (WS): Using CC, k4, sl m, p to last m, sl m, k4. Cut CC.

Next row (RS): Loosely bring up MC from two rows below and k all sts.

Next row (WS): K4, sl m, p to last m, sl m, k4.

Change to smaller circular needles and work 6 rows in garter stitch, knitting every row and adding final buttonhole row as needed. BO all sts knitwise.

Sweater sleeves (make two)

Using how-to photographs for reference, return held sts of first sleeve to larger double pointed needles, evenly distributing sts on each of three needles and using the fourth as your working needle.

Round 1: Attach MC yarn and k all sts. Pick up one st in gap between first and last sleeve sts and join to begin working in the round (31 [34, 36, 38, 40] sts).

Rounds 2–4: Knit.

Round 5: k1, k2tog, k around until 3 sts rem, ssk, k1.

(Work 9 [12, 10, 12, 13] rounds even, then repeat decrease round) 2 (2, 3, 3 3) times. 25 [28, 28, 30, 32] sts remain.

Work even until sleeve measures 4 (5, 6, 7, 7.5)" long. Do not cut MC; join CC and k 2 rounds.

Cut CC. Loosely bring up MC from 2 rounds below and k2 rounds even.

Change to smaller circular needles and work 3 ridges in garter stitch as follows: (k1 round, p 1 round) three times. BO all sts knitwise.

Weave in ends, taking care to close up any small holes that may remain at underarms. Wash and block gently to finished measurements.

KNITTING SLEEVES IN THE ROUND ON DOUBLE-POINTED NEEDLES

1: Carefully slide larger double-pointed needle into the first third of held sts, leaving holder in place if possible. Take care to insert needle as if to purl to prevent twisting your sts.

2: Once first third of sts have been picked up, slide these sts to center of first double pointed needle to secure them. Continue to pick up sts with second double pointed needle, then third, until all sts have been picked up, taking care to slide sts to center of each needle. Remove stitch holder.

3: After joining yarn and knitting around held sts, pick up one st in gap between first and last sleeve sts by inserting left hand needle from front to back through body fabric below.

4: Using right hand needle, knit into lifted st. This will be the last st of the round. Join to begin working in the round.

Difficulty Level

Finished Size
Women's Medium (9" long, 7"
circumference, unstretched)

Yarn
Cascade Bentley (75% Acrylic, 25%
Superwash Wool; 207 yd [200 m]/100
g): #05 Watermelon (MC), 1 skein; #11
Lime (CC), 1 skein.

Needles
Size 7 (4.5 mm) set of 5 double-pointed
or size needed to obtain gauge

Notions
Stitch markers; stitch holders or scrap
yarn; tapestry needle; scissors.

Gauge
20 stitches, 26 rounds = 4" in stockinette
stitch

Glossary of Abbreviations
BO – bind off
CC – contrast color
CO – cast on
k – knit
m – marker, markers
M1L – Make one left: Using left hand
needle, lift up bar between stitches from
front to back. Knit lifted bar through the
back loop to create a twist and prevent
a hole.
M1R – Make one right: Using left hand
needle, lift up bar between stitches from
back to front. Knit lifted bar through the
front loop to create a twist and prevent
a hole.
MC – main color
p – purl
pm – place marker
rep – repeat
st st – stockinette stitch
st, sts – stitch, stitches
WS – wrong side

Bright Stripe Fingerless Gloves

Knit a pair of fingerless gloves for Mom, using a bright
and cheerful shade of this fun, rainbow tweed yarn!
Throw in a contrasting stripe to match baby, or something
altogether new. These mitts are simple to knit, fun to
wear, and just the thing to let Mom know you're thinking
of her!

Notes
One skein of each color is sufficient for
2 pairs of identical fingerless gloves.
Swap the color assignments to create an
additional 2 pairs!

Pattern (Make 2)
Using MC and the long tail cast-on
method, CO 36 sts.
Divide around 3 or 4 needles according
to preference and join to begin knitting
in the round. (p1 round, k1 round) twice.
K 2 rounds even.
Leave MC hanging on WS of work, join
CC, and k 2 rounds. Cut CC.
Loosely draw up MC and continue
working in the round until work
measures 3.75" from CO edge.
Begin increasing for thumb gusset: k17,
pm, M1R, k2, M1L, pm, k to end.
Work 2 rounds even.
Next round: k to m, sl m, M1R, k to next
m, M1L, sl m, k to end.
Rep last three rounds 4 times more (14
thumb sts total).
Work 2 rounds even.
Next round: k to m, remove m, slip next

14 sts onto scrap yarn or stitch holder,
remove m, CO 2 sts, k to end.
Work even in st st until work measures
8.75" from CO edge.
P 1 round, k 1 round, p 1 round.
BO all sts knitwise.
Return held thumb sts to needles, join
yarn, and k 14 sts. Pick up 2 sts in gap
and join to begin working in the round.
Work 1 round even.
Decrease round: k1, k2tog, k until 3 sts
rem, ssk, k1.
Continue working even until thumb
measures 1" from thumb divide or
desired length, then p 1 round, k 1
round, p 1 round.
BO all sts knitwise. Weave in ends,
taking care to close up any small holes
that may remain at thumb divide.
Wash and block gently to finished
measurements.

MAKE ONE LEFT AND RIGHT

1: Make one left: Using left hand needle, lift up bar between stitches from front to back.

2: Knit lifted bar through the back loop to create a twist and prevent a hole.

3: Make one right: Using left hand needle, lift up bar between stitches from back to front.

4: Knit lifted bar through the front loop to create a twist and prevent a hole.

Difficulty Level

Finished Size
3 (6, 12, 18, 24) months

Yarn
Cascade Bentley (75% Acrylic, 25% Superwash Wool; 207 yd [200 m]/100 g): #11 Lime (MC), 1 skein; #02 Tangerine (CC), 1 skein.

Needles
Sizes 5 (3.75 mm) and 7 (4.5 mm) set of 4 double-pointed or sizes needed to obtain gauge

Notions
Stitch marker, tapestry needle; scissors.

Gauge
24 stitches, 28 rounds = 4" in stockinette stitch on smaller needles

Stitch Guide
K2, P2 rib (worked in the round)
Round 1: (k2, p2) around all sts. Rep this round for length directed.

Glossary of Abbreviations
CC – contrast color
CO – cast on
k – knit
k2tog – knit two stitches together (decrease)
m – marker, markers
MC – main color
p – purl
rem – remain
rep – repeat
RS – right side
sl – slip as if to purl
ssk – slip first stitch as if to knit, slip next stitch as if to knit, insert left hand needle through the fronts of both slipped sts and knit together (decrease)
st st – stockinette stitch
st, sts – stitch, stitches
WS – wrong side

Bright Stripe Baby Socks

Bright and bold basics are perfect for mixing and matching – like this fun, rainbow tweed yarn, set off with contrasting stripes! Baby will love these cozy, cheerful socks, knit to match or contrast with the Bright Stripe Cardigan!

Notes
Larger needles are used only when casting on, to ensure that the cuff is stretchy and not too tight for baby!

Pattern (Make 2)
Using MC, larger needles, and long tail method, CO 24 (28, 32, 28, 28) sts. Divide around 3 needles and join to beg knitting in the round. Change to smaller needles and (p 1 round, k 1 round) twice. Work 3 (3, 5, 5, 5) rounds in (k2, p2) rib. Leave MC hanging on WS of work, join CC, and k 1 round. Work 1 round in (k2, p2) rib, then cut CC. Loosely draw up MC and k 1 round. Work 5 (5, 7, 7, 7) rounds in (k2, p2) rib.
Begin heel flap: k 12 (14, 16, 14, 14) sts, arranging 6 (7, 8, 7, 7) sts on first needle and 6 (7, 8, 7, 7) sts on second needle. The remaining 12 (14, 16, 14, 14) sts will sit unworked on a third needle while the heel flap is knit and the heel is turned. Turn work and sl1, p11 (13, 15, 13, 13). Turn and sl1, k11 (13, 15, 13, 13). Rep last two rows 4 (5, 5, 6, 6) times more, ending on a RS row (11 [13, 13, 15, 15] total rows on heel flap).

Turn heel (WS)
Row 1: P6 (7, 8, 7, 7) p2tog, p1, turn.
Row 2: Sl1, k2, ssk, k1, turn.
Row 3: Sl1, p3, p2tog, p1, turn.
Row 4: Sl1, k4, ssk, k1, turn.
Row 5: Sl1, p5, p2tog, p0 (1, 1, 1, 1) turn.
Row 6 (sizes 6 months and up only): Sl1, k6, ssk, kX (0, 1, 0, 0) (6 [8, 10, 8, 8] sts rem on heel).
Continuing on the RS with the same needle, pick up 6 (8, 8, 9, 9) sts along edge of heel flap. Using new needle, k 12 (14, 16, 14, 14) held sts from needle 3. Using new needle, pick up 6 (8, 8, 9, 9) sts along other edge of heel flap, then k4 (4, 5, 4, 4) from heel sts. Place marker for beginning of round and resume working in the round (10 [12, 13, 13, 13] sts on needle 1, 12 [14, 16, 14, 14] sts on needle 2, 10 [12, 13, 13, 13] sts on needle 3). K 1 round even.

Shape heel gusset
Round 1: K until 3 sts rem on needle 1, then k2tog, k1. K across all sts on needle 2. On needle 3, k1, ssk, k to end.
Round 2: K all sts.
Rep last two rounds until 6 (7, 8, 7, 7) sts rem on needles 1 and 3 (24, 28, 32, 28, 28 sts in total). Work even in st st until work measures 2.75 (3, 3.5, 4.25, 4.5)" from heel.

Shape toe

Round 1: K until 3 sts rem on needle 1, then k2tog, k1. On needle 2, k1, ssk, k until 3 sts rem, k2tog, k1. On needle 3, k1, ssk, k to end.

Round 2: K all sts.

Rep last two rounds twice more (12, 16, 20, 16, 16 sts rem).

Work dec round only 1 (2, 3, 2, 2) times more (8 sts rem). k2.

Cut yarn leaving a 12" tail. Thread through tapestry needle and either draw through remaining sts and pull tight to close, or work Kitchener Stitch to graft toe sts together. Weave in ends, taking care to close up any small holes that may remain at toe. Wash and block gently to finished measurements.

KITCHENER STITCH FOR GRAFTING TOE

1: Arrange remaining sts so there are 4 sts on front needle and 4 sts on back needle. Thread yarn tail through tapestry needle and hold work with both knitting needles in left hand, yarn coming off the back needle.

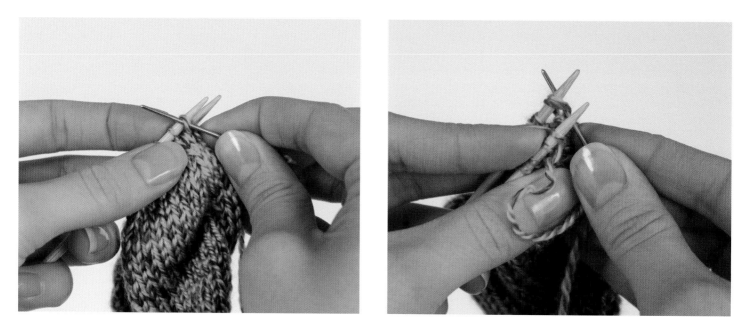

2: Setup for Kitchener Stitch by inserting tapestry needle through first stitch on front needle as if to purl and leaving stitch on the knitting needle, then through first stitch on rear needle as if to knit and leaving stitch on the knitting needle.

3: Begin working Kitchener Stitch rhythm, inserting tapestry needle through first stitch on front needle as if to knit and dropping it off knitting needle, then into second stitch (now "new" first stitch) on front needle as if to purl and leaving it on the knitting needle.

4: Finish Kitchener Stitch rhythm, inserting tapestry needle through first stitch on rear needle as if to purl and dropping it off knitting needle, then into second stitch (now "new" first stitch" on rear needle as if to knit and leaving it on the knitting needle. Repeat steps in images 3 and 4 until all sts have been worked.

Blue Jager

Baby Blanket

Cowl

Baby Hat

Baby Sweater

Difficulty Level

Finished Size
28" wide, 33" long

Yarn
Cascade 128 Superwash (100%
Superwash Merino; 128 yd [117 m]/
100 g): # 1910 Summer Sky Heather,
5 hanks.

Needles
Size 10 ½ (6.5 mm) 24" circular or size
needed to obtain gauge

Notions
Stitch markers; tapestry needle; scissors.

Gauge
15 stitches, 21 rows = 4" in stockinette
stitch

Glossary of Abbreviations
BO – bind off
CO – cast on
k – knit
m – marker, markers
p – purl
rep – repeat
pm – place marker
RS – right side
sl – slip
sts – stitches
WS – wrong side

Blue Jager Baby Blanket

Create an heirloom baby blanket using simple knits and purls! Cozy superwash merino wool makes this piece an easy care, hard wearing favorite sure to stand the test of time … and toddlers!

Notes
Pattern uses nearly all 5 skeins of yarn. Consider purchasing an additional "safety skein" if you are concerned about obtaining correct gauge.

Pattern
Using long-tail method, CO 111 sts.

Seed Stitch Border
Row 1 (WS): (k1, p1) across.
Row 2 (RS): (k1, p1) across.
Rows 3–7: Rep rows 1 and 2.

Jager Block Bottom Border
Row 1 (RS): (k1, p1) 3 times, pm, work 18-stitch repeat of row 1 of Jager Chart 5 times, then chart stitches 19–27, pm, (k1, p1) 3 times.
Row 2 (WS): (k1, p1) 3 times, sl m, work row 2 of Jager Chart stitches 27–19, work 18-stitch repeat 5 times, sl m, (k1, p1) 3 times.
Continuing as established, complete chart through row 26 ending on a WS row. Continue on to instructions for Blanket Body.

Blanket Body
Row 1 (RS): (k1, p1) 3 times, sl m, work stitches 1–18 of row 1 of Jager Chart

once, pm, (k1, p1) 31 times, p1, pm, work stitches 19–27 of row 1 of Jager Chart once, sl m, (k1, p1) 3 times.
Row 2: (k1, p1) 3 times, sl m, work stitches 27–19 of row 2 of Jager Chart once, sl m, (k1 p1) to one st before next m, p1, sl m, work stitches 18–1 of row 2 of Jager Chart once, sl m, (k1, p1) 3 times.
Row 3: (k1, p1) 3 times, sl m, work stitches 1–18 of row 3 of Jager Chart once, sl m, k1, p1, knit across center 59 sts to 2 sts before next m, p1, k1, sl m, work stitches 19–27 of row 3 of Jager Chart once, sl m, (k1, p1) 3 times.
Row 4: (k1, p1) 3 times, sl m, work stitches 27–19 of row 4 of Jager Chart once, sl m, k1, p1, purl across center 59 sts to 2 sts before next m, p1, k1, sl m, work stitches 18–1 of row 3 of Jager Chart once, sl m, (k1, p1) 3 times.
Continuing as established and maintaining stockinette stitch in center of blanket, complete 26 row repeat of Jager Chart 4 times, then rows 1–11 once more ending on a RS row.
Row 116 (WS): (k1, p1) 3 times, sl m, work stitches 27–19 of row 12 of Jager Chart once, sl m, (k1 p1) to one st before next m, p1, sl m, work stitches 18–1 of row 12 of Jager Chart once, sl

m, (k1, p1) 3 times.

Row 117: (k1, p1) 3 times, sl m, work stitches 1–18 of row 13 of Jager Chart once, sl m, (k1, p1) 31 times, p1, sl m, work stitches 19–27 of row 13 of Jager Chart once, sl m, (k1, p1) 3 times.

Jager Block Top Border

Row 1 (RS): (k1, p1) 3 times, pm, work 18-stitch repeat of row 1 of Jager Chart 5 times, then chart stitches 19–27, pm, (k1, p1) 3 times.

Row 2 (WS): (k1, p1) 3 times, sl m, work row 2 of Jager Chart stitches 27–19,

work 18-stitch repeat 5 times, sl m, (k1, p1) 3 times.

Continuing as established, complete chart through row 26 ending on a WS row.

Seed Stitch Border

Row 1 (RS): (k1, p1) across.
Row 2 (WS): (k1, p1) across.
Rows 3–7: Rep rows 1 and 2.

BO all stitches knitwise. Weave in ends, then wash and block gently to finished measurements.

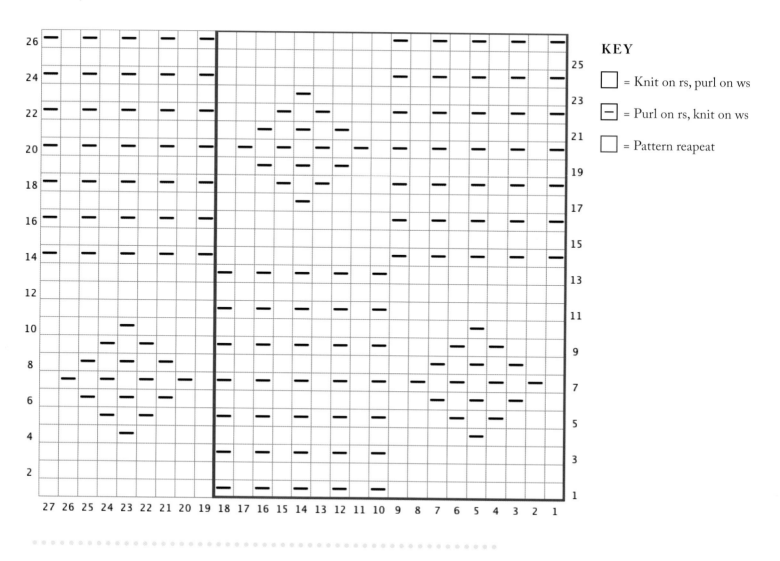

KEY

☐ = Knit on rs, purl on ws

⊟ = Purl on rs, knit on ws

☐ = Pattern reapeat

LONG TAIL CAST ON

1: Pull out a long length of yarn, approximately three times the width of your finished project measurements. Tie a slip knot and place onto knitting needle; note that this counts as your first stitch.

2: Tension yarn so that tail is over thumb and working end is over index finger, while remaining three fingers hold tightly to both ends.

3: Sliding the needle up your thumb from hand to thumbnail, grab a loop from the thumb,

4: then rotate needle tip over the strand held by your index finger,

5: then lift thumb loop over and off the needle. One stitch completed. Re-tension yarn as needed and continue casting on the given number of stitches.

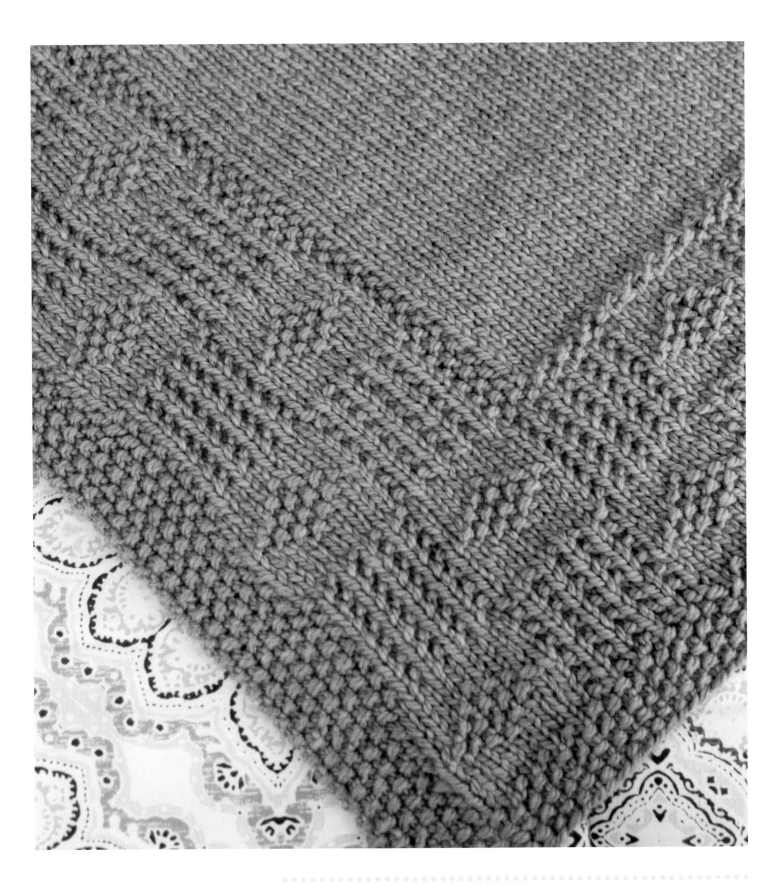

Finished Size
Small: 26" circumference, 6" deep; Large: 52" circumference, 6" deep

Yarn
Cascade 128 Superwash (100% Superwash Merino; 128 yd [117 m]/100 g): #1910 Summer Sky Heather, 1 (2) hanks.

Needles
Size 10 ½ (6.5 mm) 24" circular or size needed to obtain gauge

Notions
Stitch markers; tapestry needle; scissors.

Gauge
15 stitches, 21 rows = 4" in stockinette stitch

Glossary of Abbreviations
BO – bind off
CO – cast on
k – knit
m – marker, markers
p – purl
rep – repeat
pm – place marker
RS – right side
sl – slip
sts – stitches
Pattern

Blue Jager Cowl

Coziness abounds in this merino cowl, featuring elegant diamonds and seed stitch. Knitting in the round makes it a quick gift to knit and give! Mom will be touched you remembered her. Knit this cowl to coordinate with baby's blanket, hat and sweater for the perfect ensemble!

Pattern
Using long-tail method, CO 90 (180) sts. Pm and join to begin knitting in the round.

Seed stitch border:
Round 1: (p1, k1) around.
Round 2: (k1, p1) around.
Rounds 3–7: Rep rounds 1 and 2.

Begin Jager Block Pattern
Round 1: Work 18-stitch repeat of round 1 of Jager Chart 5 (10) times.
Round 2: Work 18-stitch repeat of round 2 of Jager Chart 5 (10) times.
Continue as established, completing chart through round 26. Cowl is now two blocks high.

Seed stitch border
Round 1: (k1, p1) around.
Round 2: (p1, k1) around.
Rounds 3–7: Rep rounds 1 and 2.
BO all stitches knitwise. Weave in ends, then wash and block gently to finished measurements.

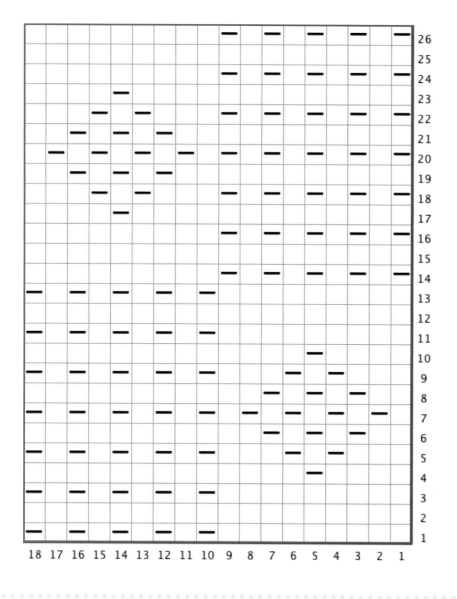

KEY

☐ = Knit

⊟ = Purl

☐ = Pattern reapeat

1: With right side of work facing, roll the edge of the cowl towards you until you can clearly see the V-shaped bound off stitches.

2: Thread tail onto tapestry needle. Skip the first V-shaped stitch of bound off edge and insert needle under both legs of the following stitch from front to back.

3: Loosely draw yarn through, then insert needle into the heart of the last bound off stitch, where the tail originated.

4: Gently tighten yarn, adjusting tension until the size of the "stitch" just made matches the other bound off stitches. It should seamlessly bridge the gap between the first and last bound off stitches. Weave in ends on WS of work.

Difficulty Level

Finished Size
3-6 (6-12, 18-24) months, 11.75 (14,
16.5" circumference, unstretched).
Sample shown is 6-12 months.

Yarn
Cascade 128 Superwash (100%
Superwash Merino; 128 yd [117 m]/100
g): #1910 Summer Sky Heather, 1 hank.

Needles
Size 9 (5.5 mm) double-pointed or size
needed to obtain gauge

Notions
Stitch marker; tapestry needle; scissors.

Gauge
17 stitches, 24 rounds = 4" (10 cm) in
stockinette stitch

Glossary of Abbreviations
CO – cast on
cdd – centered double decrease: slip next
two sts together as if to knit, knit next st,
pass two slipped stitches over.
k – knit
k2tog – knit two stitches together
p – purl
rem – remain
rep – repeat
pm – place marker
sts – stitches
WS – wrong side

Blue Jager Baby Hat

**Simple knits and purls transform into elegant diamonds
in this sweet baby hat! Knit in a cozy, washable merino
yarn, this hat is sure to become a favorite for mother and
baby alike.**

Pattern
Using long-tail method, CO 50 (60, 70)
sts. Pm and join to begin knitting in the
round.
Round 1: (P1, k1) around.
Round 2: Knit.
Rounds 3-6: Rep rounds 1 and 2.
Work rounds 1-14 of chart 5 (6, 7) times
around hat.
Rep chart rounds 13 and 14 until hat
measures 4.25 (4.75, 5.25") from CO
edge, ending after round 14 (plain knit
round).

Begin decreasing
Round 1: (P1, k3, cdd, k3) around. 40
(48, 56) sts rem.
Rounds 2, 4, 6: Knit.
Round 3: (P1, k2, cdd, k2) around. 30
(36, 42) sts rem.
Round 5: (P1, k1, cdd, k1) around. 20
(24, 28) sts rem.
Round 7: (P1, cdd) around. 10 (12, 14)
sts rem.
Round 8: (K2tog) around. 5 (6, 7) sts
rem.

Finishing
Break yarn and thread through tapestry
needle. Draw through remaining
stitches twice and pull tight. Take yarn
to WS of work and weave in all ends.
Wash and block gently to finished
measurements.

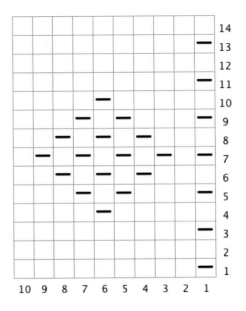

KEY

☐ = Knit

⊟ = Purl

CENTERED DOUBLE DECREASE

1: Slip next two stitches together as if to knit.

2: Knit next stitch.

3: Pass two slipped stitches over.

4: The center stitch of the three has risen to the front of the work.

Difficulty Level

Finished Size
3 (6, 12, 18, 24) months. Shown in size 12 months, modeled on a 22 pound baby.

Yarn
Cascade 128 Superwash (100% Superwash Merino; 128 yd [117 m]/100 g): #1910 Summer Sky Heather, 2 (2, 3, 3, 4) hanks.

Needles
Size 10 (6 mm) 24" circular, 16" circular, and set of 5 double-pointed or size needed to obtain gauge

Notions
Stitch markers; stitch holders or scrap yarn; tapestry needle; scissors.

Gauge
16 stitches, 23 rounds = 4" in stockinette stitch

Glossary of Abbreviations
BO – bind off
CO – cast on
k – knit
m – marker, markers
m1L – Make one left: Using left hand needle, lift up bar between stitches from front to back. Knit lifted bar through the back loop to create a twist and prevent a hole.
m1R – Make one right: Using left hand needle, lift up bar between stitches from back to front. Knit lifted bar through the front loop to create a twist and prevent a hole.
p – purl
pm – place marker
rep – repeat
RS – right side
sl – slip
st st – stockinette stitch
st, sts – stitch, stitches
WS – wrong side

Blue Jager Baby Sweater

Diamonds grace the body of this baby sweater, designed to perfectly coordinate with baby's hat and blanket. Simple raglan shaping makes for a comfortable, loose fit sure to please baby. Knit in a cozy, washable merino yarn, this sweater is warm and easy care – Mom will love to keep it handy for chilly fall days!

Notes
Sweater body and sleeves are worked in the round from the bottom up, then joined to create the yoke of the sweater. The first few rounds after joining will be quite tight; this is normal, and will become easier to knit once the raglan shaping is established.

Stitch Patterns
Stockinette Stitch (worked in the round)
Round 1 and all following rounds (RS): knit.

Pattern
Sweater body
Using long-tail method and shorter circular needles, CO 70 (70, 80, 80, 90) sts. Pm and join to begin knitting in the round.
Round 1: (p1, k1) around.
Round 2: Knit.
Rounds 3-6: Rep rounds 1 and 2.
Work 10-stitch repeat of Jager Chart 8 times around, repeating rounds 1-10 until sweater measures approximately 5.5 (5.75, 6.5, 7.5, 8)" from cast on edge. Do not cut yarn. Make note of which round of chart has just been completed and set sweater body aside.

Sweater sleeves (make two)
Using long-tail method and double-pointed needles, CO 22 (24, 26, 28, 30) sts. Pm and join to begin knitting in the round.
Round 1: (p1, k1) around.
Round 2: Knit.
Rounds 3-6: Rep rounds 1 and 2.
Size 3 months only: proceed to Round 11.
Rounds 7-10: Knit 4 rounds even in st st.
Round 11: Increase round: K1, m1L, k around until 1 st before m, m1R, k1. Two sts increased.
Rep rounds 7-11 5 (5, 6, 5, 6) more times, then knit 0 (0, 2, 7, 3) rounds even. 34 (36, 40, 40, 44) sts after increases are complete.
Cut yarn leaving a 12" tail and transfer stitches to a holder or scrap yarn. Set aside and make second identical sleeve.

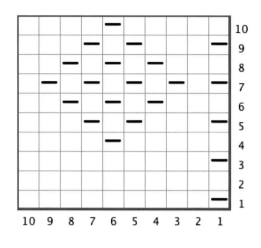

Sweater yoke

Sizes 3, 6, and 24 months only: Using longer circular needles to knit, begin by removing beginning of round marker. Work 3 sts in pattern, then replace beginning of round marker. From this point forward, treat chart stitch 4 as the first stitch of the round. Continue with directions for joining round. Joining round: Using longer circular needles, work first two sts from sweater body in pattern. Transfer these sts to a stitch holder, then work across 32 (32, 37, 37, 42) body sts in pattern, pm. Pick up first sleeve and transfer first two sleeve sts to a stitch holder. Knit around sleeve until two sts remain, pm, then slip these two sts to the same holder as the first two sleeve sts. Transfer next three body sts to a stitch holder, then work across 32 (32, 37, 37, 42) body sts in pattern, pm. Pick up second sleeve and transfer first two sleeve sts to a stitch holder. Knit around sleeve until two sts remain, pm, then slip these two sts to the same holder as the first two sleeve sts. Transfer remaining body st to same stitch holder as first two

body sts from beginning of round, then pm on circular needle for beginning of round.

Work one round even, maintaining Jager Chart pattern on body and st st on sleeves. Decrease round: (K1, k2tog, work in pattern to three sts before next m, ssk, k1, slip m) four times around. 8 sts decreased. Rep last two rounds until 52 (56, 58, 66, 68) sts remain, changing to shorter circular needles or double-pointed when there are too few sts to comfortably stretch around longer circular needles. Work 0 (2, 0, 2, 0) rounds even.

Sweater collar

Knit one round even.
Round 1: (p1, k1) around.
Round 2: Knit.
Rounds 3-6: Rep rounds 1 and 2.
BO all sts knitwise. Weave in ends and graft underarm sts together using kitchener stitch or three-needle bind off, taking care to close up any small holes that may remain from joining round. Wash and block gently to finished measurements.

KEY

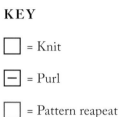

☐ = Knit

⊟ = Purl

☐ = Pattern reapeat

MAKE ONE LEFT AND RIGHT

1: Make one left: Using left hand needle, lift up bar between stitches from front to back.

2: Knit lifted bar through the back loop to create a twist and prevent a hole.

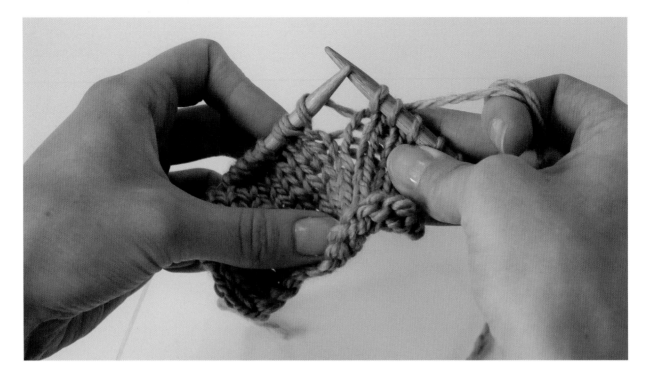

3: Make one right: Using left hand needle, lift up bar between stitches from back to front.

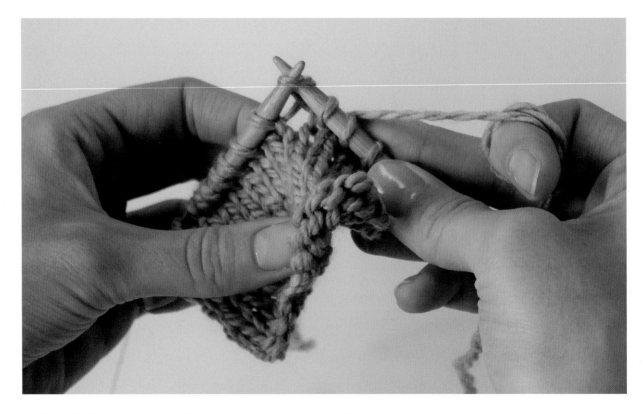

4: Knit lifted bar through the front loop to create a twist and prevent a hole.

Ropes and Rings

Difficulty Level

Finished Size
3–6 (6–12, 18–24) months; 12 (14, 17)" circumference, gently stretched. Sample shown is size 18–24 months, modeled with 2.5" of negative ease.

Yarn
Cascade Sateen Worsted (100% Acrylic; 225 yd [206 m]/100 g): #21 Cream, 1 skein.

Needles
Size 7 (4.5 mm) set of 5 double-pointed

Notions
Stitch marker; cable needle; tapestry needle; scissors.

Gauge
20 stitches, 27 rounds = 4" in stockinette stitch
26 stitches, 32 rounds = 4" in cable pattern

Glossary of Abbreviations
2/2 right leaning cable – slip first two sts to cable needle and hold to back, knit two sts from LH needle, then knit two sts from cable needle.
2/2 left leaning cable – slip first two sts to cable needle and hold to front, knit two sts from LH needle, then knit two sts from cable needle.
CO – cast on
k – knit
k2tog – knit two stitches together
kfb – knit into the front and back of next stitch (increase)
LH – left hand
m – marker
p – purl
pm – place marker
rep – repeat
RH – right hand
sl – slip
st, sts – stitch, stitches
WS – wrong side

Ropes and Rings Baby Hat

This classic cap is an excellent skill building project, featuring increases, decreases, and simple cables. Knit one to match the Ropes & Rings set, then knit a whole pile in lots of bright shades for your favorite kiddos!

Stitch Patterns
k2, p2 rib (in the round)
Round 1 and all following rounds: (k2, p2) around.

Cable Pattern
See chart, or follow below:
Rounds 1–3: (k4, p1) around.
Round 4: (2/2 right leaning cable, p1, 2/2 left leaning cable, p1) around.
Rep rounds 1–4 as directed.

Pattern
Using cable method, CO 64 (72, 84) sts, pm and join to begin knitting in the round. Work even in k2, p2 rib for 1". Knit next round, increasing 16 (18, 26) sts evenly using the kfb method. Purl one round, knit one round, purl one round.
Begin cable pattern, repeating chart rounds 1–4 until work measures 4.25 (5, 5.5)" from cast on edge, ending after round 3.
Setup to begin decreasing for crown: k4, k2tog, (k3, k2tog) around until 1 st remains. Sl this st to RH needle, remove m, return slipped st to LH needle, k2tog, replace m (64 [72, 88] sts remain). Knit one round even. Continue decreasing as follows:

Round 1: (k6, k2tog) around.
Rounds 2, 4, 6: k around.
Round 3: (k5, k2tog) around.
Round 5: (k4, k2tog) around.
Round 7: (k3, k2tog) around.
Round 8: (k2, k2tog) around.
Round 9: (k1, k2tog) around. 8 (9, 11) sts remain.
Round 10: k2tog around.
Break yarn and draw through remaining sts. Pull tightly to close hole at top of hat, then thread yarn to WS of work and weave in all ends. Block lightly to finished measurements.

WORKING A CABLE USING A CABLE NEEDLE
(EXAMPLE IS LEFT-LEANING CABLE)

1: Work in pattern to beginning of cable, taking yarn to back of work as if to knit.

2: Slip first two stitches on left hand needle to cable needle as if to purl, without twisting. Let these stitches rest in the center of the cable needle, to the front of the work.

3: Knit the next two stitches on the left hand needle as usual.

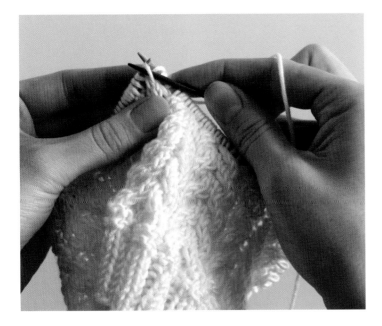

4: Return the stitches on the cable needle to the left hand needle, once again without twisting. They are now ready to be knit as usual, resulting in a completed cable. To work a right-leaning cable, repeat all steps as above, holding the cable needle to the back of the work.

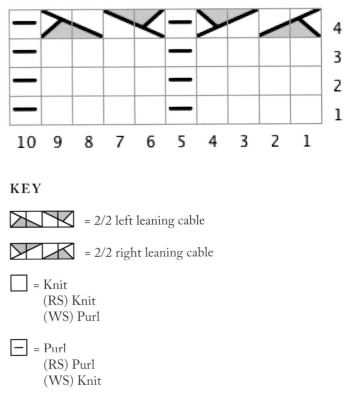

KEY

▨◩◪ = 2/2 left leaning cable

◪◩▨ = 2/2 right leaning cable

☐ = Knit
(RS) Knit
(WS) Purl

⊟ = Purl
(RS) Purl
(WS) Knit

Difficulty Level

Finished Size
26" wide, 31" long

Yarn
Cascade Sateen Worsted (100% Acrylic; 225 yd [206 m]/100 g): #21 Cream, 3 skeins.

Needles
Size 7 (4.5 mm) 29" or longer circular

Notions
Stitch markers; cable needle; tapestry needle; scissors.

Gauge
19 stitches, 26 rows = 4" in stockinette stitch
30 stitches, 28 rows = 4" in cable pattern

Glossary of Abbreviations
2/2 right leaning cable – slip first two sts to cable needle and hold to back, knit two sts from LH needle, then knit two sts from cable needle.
2/2 left leaning cable – slip first two sts to cable needle and hold to front, knit two sts from LH needle, then knit two sts from cable needle.
2/1 right leaning cable – slip first st to cable needle and hold to back, knit two sts from LH needle, then purl st from cable needle.
2/1 left leaning cable – slip first two sts to cable needle and hold to front, purl st from LH needle, then knit two sts from cable needle.
CO – cast on
k – knit
k2tog – knit two stitches together (decrease)
kfb – knit into the front and back of next stitch (increase)
m – marker
p – purl
pm – place marker
RS – right side
sl – slip
st, sts – stitch, stitches
WS – wrong side

Ropes and Rings Baby Blanket

Cozy soft and perfectly coordinated, this classic cabled blanket is updated with sharp garter stitch borders and the latest washable yarn. Two columns of cables create an elegant look while keeping this a quick-knit blanket!

Notes
Slip the first st of every row as if to knit to create a clean, crisp edge on your blanket.

Stitch Patterns
Garter Stitch (worked flat)
All rows: knit.

Cable Pattern
See chart, or follow below:
Row 1 (RS): p2, k4, p1, k4, p4, k4, p4, k4, p1, k4, p2
Row 2 (WS): k2, p4, k1, p4, k4, p4, k4, p4, k1, p4, k2
Row 3: p2, 2/2 right leaning cable, p1, 2/2 left leaning cable, p4, 2/2 right leaning cable, p4, 2/2 right leaning cable, p1, 2/2 left leaning cable, p2
Row 4: k2, p4, k1, p4, k4, p4, k4, p4, k1, p4, k2
Row 5: p2, k4, p1, k4, p3, 2/1 right leaning cable, 2/1 left leaning cable, p3, k4, p1, k4, p2
Row 6: k2, p4, k1, p4, k3, p2, k2, p2, k3, p4, k1, p4, k2
Row 7: p2, 2/2 right leaning cable, p1, 2/2 left leaning cable, p2, 2/1 right leaning cable, p2, 2/1 left leaning cable, p2, 2/2 right leaning cable, p1, 2/2 left leaning cable, p2

Row 8: k2, p4, k1, p4, k2, p2, k4, p2, k2, p4, k1, p4, k2
Row 9: p2, k4, p1, k4, p1, 2/1 right leaning cable, p4, 2/1 left leaning cable, p1, k4, p1, k4, p2
Row 10: k2, p4, k1, p4, k1, p2, k6, p2, k1, p4, k1, p4, k2
Row 11: p2, 2/2 right leaning cable, p1, 2/2 left leaning cable, p1, k2, p6, k2, p1, 2/2 right leaning cable, p1, 2/2 left leaning cable, p2
Row 12: k2, p4, k1, p4, k1, p2, k6, p2, k1, p4, k1, p4, k2
Row 13: p2, k4, p1, k4, p1, 2/1 left leaning cable, p4, 2/1 right leaning cable, p1, k4, p1, k4, p2
Row 14: k2, p4, k1, p4, k2, p2, k4, p2, k2, p4, k1, p4, k2
Row 15: p2, 2/2 right leaning cable, p1, 2/2 left leaning cable, p2, 2/1 left leaning cable, p2, 2/1 right leaning cable, p2, 2/2 right leaning cable, p1, 2/2 left leaning cable, p2
Row 16: k2, p4, k1, p4, k3, p2, k2, p2, k3, p4, k1, p4, k2
Row 17: p2, k4, p1, k4, p3, 2/1 left leaning cable, 2/1 right leaning cable, p3, k4, p1, k4, p2
Row 18: k2, p4, k1, p4, k4, p4, k4, p4, k1, p4, k2
Row 19: p2, 2/2 right leaning cable,

p1, 2/2 left leaning cable, p4, 2/2 right leaning cable, p4, 2/2 right leaning cable, p1, 2/2 left leaning cable, p2

Row 20: k2, p4, k1, p4, k4, p4, k4, p4, k1, p4, k2

Pattern

Using cable method and circular needles, CO 124 sts.

K 18 rows (9 ridges in garter stitch), ending on a WS.

Next row (RS): k all sts, increasing 20 sts evenly across row using kfb method (144 sts).

Next row (WS): K all sts.

Next row (RS): Setup for borders and cables: sl 1, k7, pm, work row 1 of chart, pm, k60, pm, work row 1 of chart, pm, k8.

Next row (WS): Sl 1, k7, sl m, work row 2 of chart, sl m, p60, sl m, work row 2 of chart, sl m, k8. Working pattern as established, repeat chart rows 1–20 8 times.

Work rows 1–19 once more, ending on a RS row.

Next row (WS): K all sts.

Next row (RS): K all sts, decreasing 20 sts evenly across row using k2tog method.

K 17 rows more, ending on a WS row (10 ridges in garter stitch visible on RS).

Next row (RS): BO all sts knitwise . Cut yarn and weave in ends. Block lightly to finished measurements.

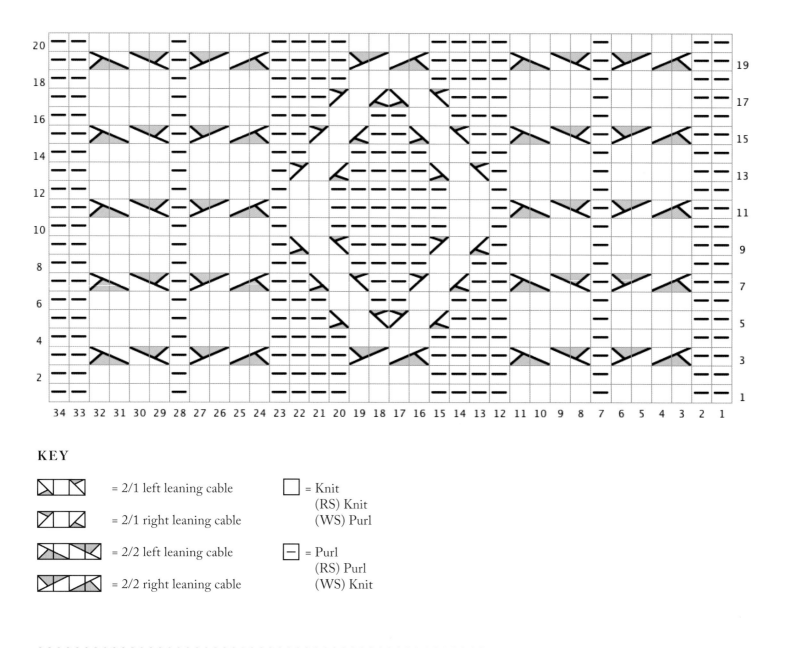

KEY

= 2/1 left leaning cable

= 2/1 right leaning cable

= 2/2 left leaning cable

= 2/2 right leaning cable

= Knit
(RS) Knit
(WS) Purl

= Purl
(RS) Purl
(WS) Knit

1: When working with a garter stitch border, try to avoid joining new yarn at the very edge as this is a difficult location to weave in ends discreetly. Instead, try to weave ends in the body of the blanket.

2: Cross the yarns so that they do not pull apart from each other and create a hole when weaving in.

3: Duplicate the flow of stitches in your chosen row carefully, and take care not to split stitches or pull too tightly as this can distort the knitting. Weaving should be nearly invisible.

4: After weaving for approximately 2", clip the end close to the fabric. When working with a slippery yarn, consider tying an overhand knot to prevent unraveling.

Difficulty Level

Finished Size
19.25 (22.5)" circumference, gently stretched. Sample shown is 22.5", modeled with 1" of negative ease.

Yarn
Cascade Sateen Worsted (100% Acrylic; 225 yd [206 m]/100 g): #21 Cream, 1 skein.

Needles
Size 7 (4.5 mm) 16" circular and set of 5 double-pointed

Notions
Stitch marker; cable needle; tapestry needle; scissors.

Gauge
20 stitches, 27 rounds = 4" in stockinette stitch
26 stitches, 32 rounds = 4" in cable pattern

Glossary of Abbreviations
2/2 right leaning cable – slip first two sts to cable needle and hold to back, knit two sts from LH needle, then knit two sts from cable needle.
2/2 left leaning cable – slip first two sts to cable needle and hold to front, knit two sts from LH needle, then knit two sts from cable needle.
2/1 right leaning cable – slip first st to cable needle and hold to back, knit two sts from LH needle, then purl st from cable needle.
2/1 left leaning cable – slip first two sts to cable needle and hold to front, purl st from LH needle, then knit two sts from cable needle.
CO – cast on
k – knit
k2tog – knit two stitches together (decrease)
kfb – knit into the front and back of next stitch (increase)

m – marker
p – purl
pm – place marker
sl – slip
ssk – slip first stitch as if to knit, slip second stitch as if to knit, then insert left hand needle through the fronts of both slipped stitches and knit them together (decrease)
st, sts – stitch, stitches
WS – wrong side

Cable Pattern
See chart, or follow below:
Rounds 1–3: (k4, p4, k4, p4, k4, p1) 6 (7) times around.
Round 4: (2/2 left leaning cable, p4, 2/2 right leaning cable, p4, 2/2 right leaning cable, p1) 6 (7) times around.
Round 5: (k4, p4, k4, p4, k4, p1) 6 (7) times around.
Round 6: (k4, p3, 2/1 right leaning cable, 2/1 left leaning cable, p3, k4, p1) 6 (7) times around.
Round 7: (k4, p3, k2, p2, k2, p3, k4, p1) 6 (7) times around.
Round 8: (2/2 left leaning cable, p2, 2/1 right leaning cable, p2, 2/1 left leaning cable, p2, 2/2 right leaning cable, p1) 6

Ropes and Rings Adult Hat

The perfect accessory for Mom or Dad! A more grown-up version of the Ropes & Rings baby hat, this timeless toque is beautifully coordinated with the set but can certainly stand alone. Take your cable knitting to the next level with this intermediate project!

(7) times around.
Round 9: (k4, p2, k2, p4, k2, p2, k4, p1) 6 (7) times around.
Round 10: (k4, p1, 2/1 right leaning cable, p4, 2/1 left leaning cable, p1, k4, p1) 6 (7) times around.
Round 11: (k4, p1, k2, p6, k2, p1, k4, p1) 6 (7) times around.
Round 12: (2/2 left leaning cable, p1, k2, p6, k2, p1, 2/2 right leaning cable, p1) 6 (7) times around.
Round 13: (k4, p1, k2, p6, k2, p1, k4, p1) 6 (7) times around.
Round 14: (k4, p1, 2/1 left leaning cable, p4, 2/1 right leaning cable, p1, k4, p1) 6 (7) times around.
Round 15: (k4, p2, k2, p4, k2, p2, k4, p1) 6 (7) times around.
Round 16: (2/2 left leaning cable, p2, 2/1 left leaning cable, p2, 2/1 right leaning cable, p2, 2/2 right leaning cable, p1) 6 (7) times around.
Round 17: (k4, p3, k2, p2, k2, p3, k4, p1) 6 (7) times around.
Round 18: (k4, p3, 2/1 left leaning cable, 2/1 right leaning cable, p3, k4, p1) 6 (7) times around.
Round 19: (k4, p4, k4, p4, k4, p1) 6 (7) times around.

Round 20: (2/2 left leaning cable, p4, 2/2 right leaning cable, p4, 2/2 right leaning cable, p1) 6 (7) times around.

Rounds 21–23: (k4, p4, k4, p4, k4, p1) 6 (7) times around.

Round 24: (2/2 left leaning cable, p4, 2/2 right leaning cable, p4, 2/2 right leaning cable, p1) 6 (7) times around.

Round 25: (k4, p4, k4, p4, k4, p1) 6 (7) times around.

Round 26: (k4, p3, 2/1 right leaning cable, 2/1 left leaning cable, p3, k4, p1) 6 (7) times around.

Round 27: (k4, p3, k2, p2, k2, p3, k4, p1) 6 (7) times around.

Round 28: (2/2 left leaning cable, p2, 2/1 right leaning cable, p2, 2/1 left leaning cable, p2, 2/2 right leaning cable, p1) 6 (7) times around.

Round 29: (k4, p2, k2, p4, k2, p2, k4, p1) 6 (7) times around.

Round 30: (k4, p1, 2/1 right leaning cable, p4, 2/1 left leaning cable, p1, k4, p1) 6 (7) times around.

Round 31: (k4, p1, k2, p6, k2, p1, k4, p1) 6 (7) times around.

Round 32: (2/2 left leaning cable, p1, k2, p6, k2, p1, 2/2 right leaning cable, p1) 6 (7) times around.

Round 33: (k4, p1, k2, p6, k2, p1, k4, p1) 6 (7) times around.

Round 34: (ssk, k2, p1, 2/1 left leaning cable, p4, 2/1 right leaning cable, p1, k2, k2tog, p1) 6 (7) times around.

Round 35: (k3, p2, k2, p4, k2, p2, k3, p1) 6 (7) times around.

Round 36: (ssk, k1, p2, 2/1 left leaning cable, p2, 2/1 right leaning cable, p2, k1, k2tog, p1) 6 (7) times around.

Round 37: (k2, p3, k2, p2, k2, p3, k2, p1) 6 (7) times around.

Round 38: (ssk, k1, p2, 2/1 left leaning cable, 2/1 right leaning cable, p2, k1, k2tog, p1) 6 (7) times around.

Round 39: (ssk, k1, p2, k4, p2, k1, k2tog, p1) 6 (7) times around.

Round 40: (ssk, k1, p1, 2/2 right leaning cable, p1, k1, k2tog, p1) 6 (7) times around.

Round 41: (ssk, k6, k2tog, p1) 6 (7) times around.

Round 42: (ssk, k4, k2tog, p1) 6 (7) times around.

Round 43: (ssk, k2, k2tog, p1) 6 (7) times around.

Round 44: (ssk, k2tog, p1) 6 (7) times around.

Move to finishing directions.

Pattern

Using cable method and circular needles, CO 96 (112) sts, pm and join to begin knitting in the round.

Work even in k2, p2 rib for 1.5".

Knit next round, increasing 30 (35) sts evenly using the kfb method (126 [147] sts).

Purl one round, knit one round, purl one round.

Work cable pattern rounds 1–44, repeating stitches 1–21 6 (7) times around and moving to double-pointed needles when work becomes too tight to fit comfortably around circular needles. Work measures approximately 8" from cast on edge.

Finishing

Work final decrease round as follows: (k2tog, p1) 6 (7) times (12 [14] sts remain).

Break yarn and draw through remaining sts. Pull tightly to close hole at top of hat, then thread yarn to WS of work and weave in all ends. Block lightly to finished measurements.

SECURING THE TOP OF A HAT

1: Break yarn leaving a 12" tail, and thread onto a yarn needle.

2: Carefully slip stitches off of knitting needles and onto yarn needle, taking care not to split your stitches.

3: Continue transferring stitches from knitting needles onto yarn needle, slipping each stitch from tip to tip as if to purl.

4: Gently tighten yarn until stitches form a round pucker at the top of the hat. Thread yarn through to back of work to secure and weave in. When using a slippery yarn, consider tying a knot to prevent unraveling.

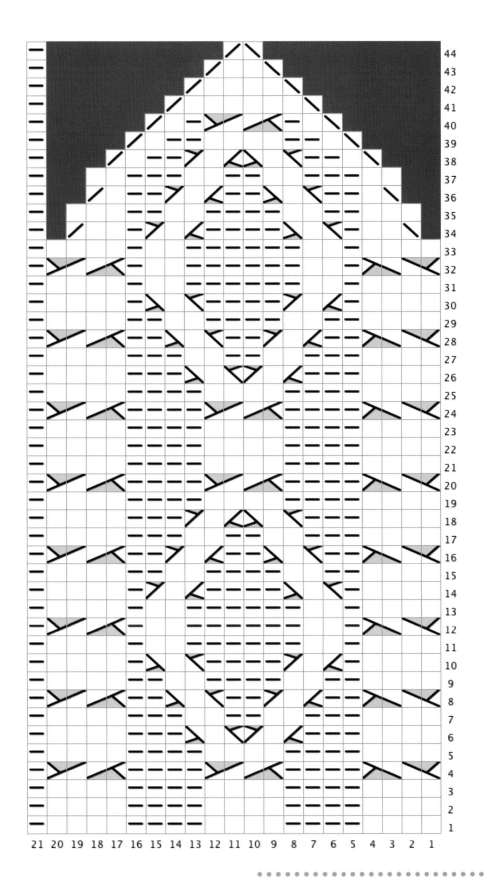

KEY

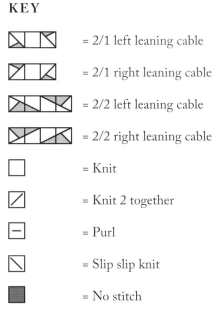

= 2/1 left leaning cable

= 2/1 right leaning cable

= 2/2 left leaning cable

= 2/2 right leaning cable

= Knit

= Knit 2 together

= Purl

= Slip slip knit

= No stitch

Difficulty Level

Finished Size
3 (6, 12, 18, 24) months. Shown in size 18 months, modeled on a 27 pound baby.

Yarn
Cascade Sateen Worsted (100% Acrylic; 225 yd [206 m]/100 g): #21 Cream, 1 (2, 2, 3, 3) skein(s).

Needles
Size 7 (4.5 mm) 24" circular and set of 5 double-pointed

Notions
22 (22, 22, 22, 24)" zipper; stitch markers; cable needle; stitch holders or scrap yarn; tapestry needle; scissors. Sample shown used Coats All Purpose Plastic Zipper #256 Natural.

Gauge
20 stitches, 26 rows = 4" in stockinette stitch worked flat
30 stitches, 28 rows = 4" in cable pattern

Glossary of Abbreviations
2/2 right leaning cable – slip first two sts to cable needle and hold to back, knit two sts from LH needle, then knit two sts from cable needle.
2/2 left leaning cable – slip first two sts to cable needle and hold to front, knit two sts from LH needle, then knit two sts from cable needle.
2/1 right leaning cable – slip first st to cable needle and hold to back, knit two sts from LH needle, then purl st from cable needle.
2/1 left leaning cable – slip first two sts to cable needle and hold to front, purl st from LH needle, then knit two sts from cable needle.
CO – cast on
k – knit
k2tog – knit two stitches together (decrease)
kfb – knit into the front and back of next stitch (increase)

LH – left hand
LR – Right leaning lifted increase: Using right hand needle, lift the stitch below the stitch on the left hand needle from the back and knit it.
m – marker
p – purl
pm – place marker
RS – right side
sl – slip
ssk – slip first stitch as if to knit, slip second stitch as if to knit, then insert left hand needle through the fronts of both slipped stitches and knit them together (decrease)
st, sts – stitch, stitches
WS – wrong side

Notes
Sweater is worked in one piece from the bottom hem to the underarm, then divided to work the fronts and backs separately. Sleeves are picked up from the armholes and knit down seamlessly in the round.
Right and left front and back directions refer to the sweater as worn.

Ropes and Rings Hoodie Sweater

Combining classic fashion with modern practicality, this washable zip-up-the-back hoodie is cozy for baby and easy on Mom! The cabled panels and nearly seamless design make for a fun and interesting project. Add the matching baby hat and blanket for a sweet bunting set, or keep it simple and pair with jeans for an outdoor adventure!

Stitch Patterns
Stockinette Stitch
Row 1 (RS): knit.
Row 2 (WS): purl.
Rep rows 1 and 2 for length stated.

Garter Stitch (worked flat)
Knit every row.
Garter Stitch (worked in the round)
Round 1: knit.
Round 2: purl.

Cable Pattern:
See chart, (p88) or follow below:
Row 1 (RS): p2, k4, p1, k4, p4, k4, p4, k4, p1, k4, p2
Row 2 (WS): k2, p4, k1, p4, k4, p4, k4, p4, k1, p4, k2
Row 3: p2, 2/2 right leaning cable, p1, 2/2 left leaning cable, p4, 2/2 right leaning cable, p4, 2/2 right leaning cable, p1, 2/2 left leaning cable, p2
Row 4: k2, p4, k1, p4, k4, p4, k4, p4, k1, p4, k2
Row 5: p2, k4, p1, k4, p3, 2/1 right leaning cable, 2/1 left leaning cable, p3, k4, p1, k4, p2

Row 6: k2, p4, k1, p4, k3, p2, k2, p2, k3, p4, k1, p4, k2

Row 7: p2, 2/2 right leaning cable, p1, 2/2 left leaning cable, p2, 2/1 right leaning cable, p2, 2/1 left leaning cable, p2, 2/2 right leaning cable, p1, 2/2 left leaning cable, p2

Row 8: k2, p4, k1, p4, k2, p2, k4, p2, k2, p4, k1, p4, k2

Row 9: p2, k4, p1, k4, p1, 2/1 right leaning cable, p4, 2/1 left leaning cable, p1, k4, p1, k4, p2

Row 10: k2, p4, k1, p4, k1, p2, k6, p2, k1, p4, k1, p4, k2

Row 11: p2, 2/2 right leaning cable, p1, 2/2 left leaning cable, p1, k2, p6, k2, p1, 2/2 right leaning cable, p1, 2/2 left leaning cable, p2

Row 12: k2, p4, k1, p4, k1, p2, k6, p2, k1, p4, k1, p4, k2

Row 13: p2, k4, p1, k4, p1, 2/1 left

leaning cable, p4, 2/1 right leaning cable, p1, k4, p1, k4, p2

Row 14: k2, p4, k1, p4, k2, p2, k4, p2, k2, p4, k1, p4, k2

Row 15: p2, 2/2 right leaning cable, p1, 2/2 left leaning cable, p2, 2/1 left leaning cable, p2, 2/1 right leaning cable, p2, 2/2 right leaning cable, p1, 2/2 left leaning cable, p2

Row 16: k2, p4, k1, p4, k3, p2, k2, p2, k3, p4, k1, p4, k2

Row 17: p2, k4, p1, k4, p3, 2/1 left leaning cable, 2/1 right leaning cable, p3, k4, p1, k4, p2

Row 18: k2, p4, k1, p4, k4, p4, k4, p4, k1, p4, k2

Row 19: p2, 2/2 right leaning cable, p1, 2/2 left leaning cable, p4, 2/2 right leaning cable, p4, 2/2 right leaning cable, p1, 2/2 left leaning cable, p2

Row 20: k2, p4, k1, p4, k4, p4, k4, p4, k1, p4, k2

Pattern

Beginning at bottom hem, using cable method and circular needles CO 96 (100, 104, 112, 116) sts. Do not join. K 7 rows in garter stitch, ending on a RS row. Next row (WS): k 24 (25, 26, 28, 29), pm for side, k 4 (5, 6, 8, 9), (k3, LR) 10 times, k 4 (5, 6, 8, 9), pm for side, k 24 (25, 26, 28, 29) (total of 106 [110, 114, 122, 126] sts).

Next row (RS): k to m, sl m, k 12 (13, 14, 16, 17) work chart row 1, k 12 (13, 14, 16, 17), sl m, k to end.

Next row (WS): k2 for garter st border (maintain k2 at either end throughout), p to m, sl m, p 12 (13, 14, 16, 17), work chart row 2, p 12 (13, 14, 16, 17), sl m, p until 2 sts rem, k2 for garter st border. Continue working last two rows, repeating cable chart rows 1–20 until work measures 6.75 (7, 7.5, 8, 8.5)" from CO edge, ending on a WS row. Take note of the last chart row worked.

Next row (RS): divide the front of the sweater from the backs as follows, removing side m as you come to them: k to 2 sts before first side m, BO next 4 sts, knit to cable panel, work first 12 sts of cable panel in pattern, BO next 10 sts (center diamond cable), work rem sts in chart pattern, k to 2 sts before second side m, BO next 4 sts, k to end. 22 (23, 24, 26, 27) sts on each back piece, and 44 (46, 48, 52, 54) sts on front.

Move front sts and left back sts to stitch holders or scrap yarn.

Right back

Maintaining garter st border at center back, continue working even in st st until work measures 11 (11.5, 12.5, 13, 14)" from CO edge, ending on a WS row. Next row (RS): BO 8 sts for shoulder, k to end. Move sts to a stitch holder or scrap yarn.

Left back

Return held sts to needles, rejoin yarn and work as for right back, ending on a WS row.

Next row (RS): k18, BO remaining 8

sts for shoulder. Move sts from knitting needle to a stitch holder or scrap yarn.

Right front

Return held sts to needles and join yarn, ready to work a WS row. Work 5 rows even in st st, ending on a WS row.
Decrease row (RS): Work chart sts, k1, ssk, k to end.
Work 3 rows even in pattern, then work decrease row.
Repeat last four rows 0 (0, 1, 1, 1) time more, then work one WS row even in pattern (19 [21, 21, 23, 24] sts remain).
Next row (RS): Work 15 sts in pattern, then BO remaining 4 (6, 6, 8, 9) sts for shoulder. Move sts from knitting needle to a stitch holder and cut yarn.

Left front

Return held sts to needles and join yarn, ready to work a WS row. Work 5 rows even in st st, ending on a WS row.
Decrease row (RS): K to 3 sts before chart, k2tog, k1, work chart sts.
Work 3 rows even in pattern, then work decrease row.
Repeat last four rows 0 (0, 1, 1, 1) time more, then work one WS row even in pattern (19 [21, 21, 23, 24] sts remain).
Next row (RS): BO 5 (7, 7, 9, 10) sts for shoulder (remaining st on RH needle will become part of hood), work remaining sts in pattern (15 sts remain). Do not cut yarn.

Left hood

Return left back sts to circular needles with left front and work 1 WS row in pattern.
Next row (RS): Increase 8 (10, 12, 12, 14) sts evenly across st st portion using LR increase method, then work even across remaining cable sts at other end. Work even in pattern until hood measures 7.5 (8, 8.5, 9, 9.5)" from increase row ending on a WS row, then move sts from knitting needle to a stitch holder. Leave a long length of yarn for joining hood seam. Sweater now measures 18.5 (19.5, 21, 22, 23.5)" from

INSTALLING A ZIPPER

1: Turn sweater inside out and lay flat. With zipper closed, align with back opening and pin in place.

cast on edge to top of hood.

Right hood

Return right front and back sts to circular needles and work 1 WS row in pattern.

Next row (RS): work even across cable sts, then increase 8 (10, 12, 12, 14) sts evenly across st st portion using LR increase method.

Work even in pattern until hood measures 7.5 (8, 8.5, 9, 9.5)" from increase row ending on a WS row, and cut yarn.

Return held sts from left hood to same circular needles as right hood or place on a double pointed needle. Hold hood halves with right sides together, wrong sides facing out. Using spare double pointed needle and long length of yarn from left hood, work 3 needle bind off to join top of hood.

Sleeves (Make 2)

Join shoulder seams. With RS facing, beginning at center of underarm bind off and using double pointed needles, pick up 42 (48, 52, 56, 60) sts (approximately 4 sts for every 5 rows) around armhole opening. Pm for beginning of round and join to begin knitting in the round.

Knit 5 rounds even.

Decrease round: k 1, k2tog, k until 3 sts remain, ssk, k1.

Repeat last 6 rounds 4 (4, 5, 6, 7) times more.

K even until sleeve measures 5 (5.5, 6.5, 7, 7.5)".

Work 8 rounds in garter stitch, then BO all sts.

Hood edging

With RS facing, beginning at right front edge just above center diamond bind off edge and using circular needles, pick up 4 sts for every 5 rows up along right front of hood, down left front of hood, and down to left front edge just above center diamond bind off. Do not join.

K 7 rows even in garter stitch (4 ridges visible on RS), then BO all sts knitwise.

Finishing

Using tapestry needle, seam front bands to cast off edge of cable chart at chest center. Weave in all ends.

Lightly steam block or wet block sweater, taking care to straighten out back opening before arranging front, hood, and sleeves. Iron any creases in zipper. When sweater is dry, install zipper by hand or sewing machine (see how-to photo tutorial). Re-block as necessary.

2: Carefully unzip sweater, taking care to keep pins in place. If machine sewing, baste zipper in place, remove pins, and sew. If hand sewing, use a backstitch to sew zipper firmly in place.

3: Stitches should be small and close to the teeth to ensure durability.

4: Zipper teeth should run just under or right along edge of knitting for cleanest look and to minimize chance of snagging.

Sweet Berries

Difficulty Level

Finished Size
30" wide, 33" long

Yarn
Cascade Longwood (100% Superwash Extrafine Merino; 191 yd [175 m]/100 g): #11 Walnut (MC), 3 hanks; #05 Peach or #22 Sky Blue (CC1), 1 hank; #01 White (CC2), 1 hank.

Needles
Size 8 (5 mm) 24" circular and 2 double-pointed

Notions
Stitch markers; approximately 1 yard of backing fabric (sample shown used washable micro fleece); sewing thread to match backing fabric; sheet of cardstock or cardboard; tapestry needle; scissors.

Gauge
19 stitches, 26 rounds = 4" in stockinette stitch

Glossary of Abbreviations
BO – bind off
CC – contrast color
CO – cast on
k – knit
m – marker
MC – main color
p – purl
pm – place marker
sl – slip
st st – stockinette stitch
st, sts – stitch, stitches
yo – yarn over

Sweet Berries Baby Blanket

This charming colorwork blanket is a breeze to knit! It is worked in the round with steek stitches, no ends to weave in, and a cozy fleece backing perfect for cuddling. Knit it up as a special heirloom or as the perfect complement to the Sweet Berries Sweater!

Notes
Blanket is knit in the round with extra stitches to allow for the cutting of a steek. All color or skein changes should be placed at the beginning of the round so that any yarn ends are cut away during steek cutting.
Edging is applied i-cord, worked after steek cutting.
Fabric backing and steek reinforcements may be sewn by machine or by hand.

Stockinette Stitch (in the round)
Round 1 and all following rounds: knit.

Pattern
Using cable method, MC and circular needles, CO 150 sts. Pm and join to begin knitting in the round.
K3, pm for left steek edge, k144, pm for right steek edge, k3.
Join CC1 and k1CC, k1MC, k1CC, sl m, work 6 repeats of round 1 of chart pattern, sl m, k1CC, k1MC, k1CC.
Continue to alternate MC and CC yarns between steek markers throughout blanket, creating columns of color on two-color rounds or bands of plain color on single-color rounds.

Continue working as established until Round 43 of chart is completed.
Join MC and work even in st st until work measures 26" from CO edge.
Rotate chart 180 degrees and work rounds 43–1 so that blanket ends are mirrored, remembering to keep steek stitches in alternating columns of color.
BO all sts knitwise using MC.

Finishing
Using sewing machine or backstitching by hand, reinforce blanket on either side of center two steek stitches so that there is a selvedge stitch between the blanket body and the reinforcement lines after cutting. Insert cardstock or cardboard into the center of the blanket to run beneath the scissors and carefully cut the blanket apart between the center steek stitches, with the lines of reinforcement on either side. All yarn ends should now be cut away, but if there are any ends remaining elsewhere in the blanket, weave them in.
Using double-pointed needles and CC1, work 4-stitch applied i-cord edging (see how-to photographs): with RS of blanket facing, beginning at any corner

and using cable method, CO 4 sts. *Knit 3 sts, slip the 4th st as if to knit, yo, then insert full needle into edge stitch or selvedge stitch of blanket, yo, and draw up a stitch in CC1. There are now 6 sts on the needle. Using tip of empty needle, lift stitches 4 and 5 over and off stitch 6. Slide all sts to the opposite end of the needle and repeat from *.

Continue working applied i-cord around circumference of blanket, working 2–3 sts into each corner st as needed to encourage the i-cord to wrap around the corner smoothly.

When entire blanket circumference has been worked, BO all sts and sew beginning of i-cord to end. Weave in ends. Block blanket to finished measurements. When dry, machine or hand sew backing to wrong side of blanket.

KEY

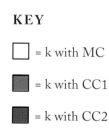 = k with MC

= k with CC1

= k with CC2

APPLIED I-CORD EDGING (4 STITCHES)

1: Knit 3 sts, slip the 4th st as if to knit, then yarn over.

2: Insert full needle into edge stitch or selvedge stitch of blanket.

3: Yarn over and draw up a stitch

4: Using tip of empty needle, lift stitches 4 and 5 over and off stitch 6.

Difficulty Level

● ● ○ ○

Finished Size
24" circumference, 8.25" deep

Yarn
Cascade Longwood (100% Superwash Extrafine Merino; 191 yd [175 m]/100 g): #05 Peach or #22 Sky Blue (MC), 1 hank; #01 White (CC), 1 hank.

Needles
Size 8 (5 mm) 24" circular

Notions
Stitch marker; tapestry needle; scissors.

Gauge
20 stitches, 24 rounds = 4" in colorwork pattern

Notes
Cowl may be made deeper by working more reps of the 6 rounds of the colorwork pattern.
Cowl may be made longer by casting on more sts in multiples of 8, then working more reps of the colorwork pattern.

Glossary of Abbreviations
BO – bind off
CC – contrast color
CO – cast on
k – knit
m – marker
MC – main color
p – purl
pm – place marker
rep – repeat
st, sts – stitch, stitches

Sweet Berries Cowl

This cheerful cowl is quick to knit and makes a fun statement piece! Choose bright shades or neutrals to match baby's ensemble.

Stitch Patterns
k2, p2 rib
Round 1 and all following rounds: (k2, p2) around.

Pattern
Using longtail method and your choice of MC, CO 120 sts. Pm and join to begin knitting in the round.
Work even in k2, p2 rib for 2".

Join CC and begin working chart, repeating sts 1–8 fifteen times around cowl.
Rep rounds 1–6 four times or until cowl measures 2" less than desired depth.
Cut CC and k one round even in MC to avoid bi-colored purls.
Work even in k2, p2 rib for 2", then BO all sts in pattern. Weave in ends and block to finished measurements.

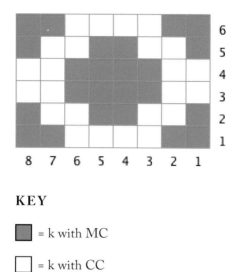

KEY

■ = k with MC

□ = k with CC

BINDING OFF IN PATTERN

1: In this example, the knitting pattern has been (k2, p2) rib. To bind off in pattern, we will continue this trend and begin by knitting two sts.

2: Pass the first st over the second to bind off.

3: Bring the working yarn to the front to purl.

4: Purl the next st, then lift the "new" first st over the second and off the right hand needle tip. The next st will be purled as well. Throughout the bind off, knit the knit sts and purl the purl sts, taking care to shift the working yarn from front to back as necessary.

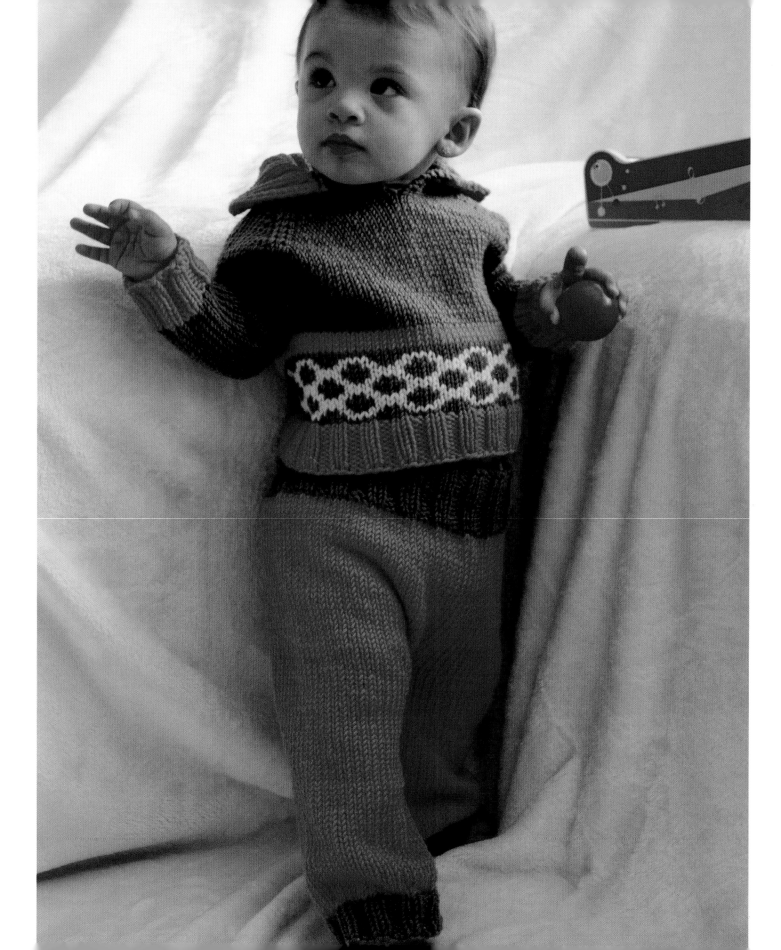

Difficulty Level

Finished Size
3 (6, 12, 18, 24) months. Sample shown is size 12 months, modeled on an 18 pound baby.

Yarn
Cascade Longwood (100% Superwash Extrafine Merino; 191 yd [175 m]/100 g): #05 Peach (MC), 1 (1, 2, 2, 2) hanks; #11 Walnut (CC), 1 hank.

Needles
Size 8 (5 mm) 16" circular and set of 5 double-pointed

Notions
Stitch marker; stitch holder or scrap yarn; tapestry needle; scissors.

Gauge
19 stitches, 26 rounds = 4" in stockinette stitch

Glossary of Abbreviations
BO – bind off
CC – contrast color
CO – cast on
k – knit
k2tog – knit two stitches together
m – marker
m1 – using left hand needle, lift up bar between stitches from front to back. Knit lifted bar through the back loop to create a twist and prevent a hole.
MC – main color
p – purl
pm – place marker
rem – remain
sl – slip
st st – stockinette stitch
st, sts – stitch, stitches

Sweet Berries Pants

These sweet pants are simple to knit and easy to care for! The generous waistband and rise are cloth diaper friendly, and legs can be easily extended to fit taller babies. For thinner babies, choose a smaller size for the waist band and follow the length directions for their age. Consider adding stripes for even more fun!

Stitch Patterns
k2, p2 rib
Round 1 and all following rounds: (k2, p2) around.
Stockinette Stitch (in the round)
Round 1 and all following rounds: knit.

Pattern
Using longtail method, circular needles and CC, CO 72 (76, 84, 88, 92) sts. PM and join to begin knitting in the round. Work even in k2, p2 rib for 2" and cut yarn.
Join MC and work increase round as follows: (k4, m1) 24 (24, 20, 20, 20) times around, k to end (96, [100, 104, 108, 112] sts).
Work even in st st for 5 (5.5, 6, 7, 8) inches (work measures 7 [7.5, 8, 9, 10] inches from cast on).
Prepare to divide legs: BO 4 sts, k 43 (45, 47, 49, 51) sts, BO next 4 sts, k rem 43 (45, 47, 49, 51) sts. Remove m and using a piece of scrap yarn or stitch holder, sl first set of 44 (46, 48, 50, 52) sts off knitting needles and set aside.
The second set of 44 (46, 48, 50, 52) sts should still have working yarn attached. Sl sts to double pointed needles, distributing evenly around 4 needles. PM and rejoin to work first leg in the round.

Work even in st st in the round until leg measures 5.75 (6.5, 7, 8, 10) inches from bind off.
Using k2tog method, dec 12 (10, 12, 10, 10) sts evenly around (32 [36, 36, 40, 40] sts rem).
Cut yarn and join CC. Knit one round even, then work in k2, p2 rib for 1.5". BO in pattern.
Return held sts to double pointed needles, rejoin yarn leaving a long tail for seaming crotch, and work second leg following the same directions for first leg.
Seam crotch gap using long tail, then weave in all ends and block.

AVOIDING BI-COLORED PURL STITCHES

1: Working in k2, p2 rib immediately following a color change creates a bi-colored purl stitch.

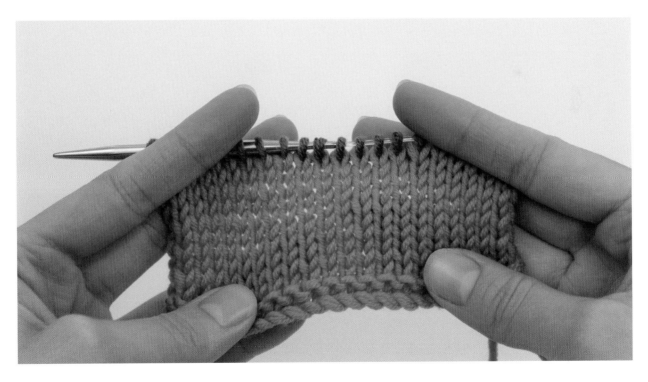

2: To avoid this problem, knit the first round of the color change.

3: Once the first round is complete, work k2, p2 rib as usual and note that the bi-colored purls have disappeared.

4: The bi-colored purl results on the wrong side of the work, where it will go unnoticed.

Difficulty Level

Finished Size
3 (6, 12, 18, 24) months. Peach sample shown is size 12 months, modeled on an 18 pound baby; blue sample shown is size 18 months, modeled on a 24 pound baby.

Yarn
Cascade Longwood (100% Superwash Extrafine Merino; 191 yd [175 m]/100 g): #11 Walnut (MC), 1 (1, 1, 2, 2) hanks; #05 Peach OR #22 Sky Blue (CC1), 1 hank; #01 White (CC2), 1 hank.

Needles
Size 8 (5 mm) 16" circular and set of 5 double-pointed

Notions
Stitch marker; stitch holder or scrap yarn; tapestry needle; scissors.

Gauge
19 stitches, 26 rounds = 4" in stockinette stitch

Glossary of Abbreviations
BO – bind off
CC – contrast color
CO – cast on
k – knit
k2tog – knit two stitches together
kfb – knit into the front and back of stitch (increase)
m – marker
MC – main color
p – purl
pm – place marker
rep – repeat
RS – right side
sl – slip
st st – stockinette stitch
st, sts – stitch, stitches
WS – wrong side

Sweet Berries Sweater

Contrasting ribbing and a simple, sweet colorwork design set this sweater apart! Choose gender neutral shades or a pop of pink or blue for that special baby. The top down design is easy to knit and can be tried on your baby as you go to ensure a perfect fit.

Stitch Patterns
k2, p2 rib (worked flat)
Row 1: (k2, p2) across, ending k2.
Row 2: (p2, k2) across, ending p2.
k2, p2 rib (in the round)
Round 1 and all following rounds: (k2, p2) around.
Stockinette Stitch (in the round)
Round 1 and all following rounds: knit.

Pattern
Using cable method, circular needles and CC1, CO 54 (58, 58, 62, 66) sts. Do not join.
Begin working back and forth in k2, p2 rib as follows:
Row 1 (RS): (k2, p2) across until 2 sts remain, k2.
Row 2 (WS): (p2, k2) across until 2 sts remain, p2.
Rep rows 1 and 2 until work measures 2.25 (2.5, 2.5, 2.75, 3)" from CO edge, ending on a RS row. Cut yarn and join MC.
Knit across all sts, decrease 14 sts evenly using the k2tog method (40 [44, 44, 48, 52] sts remain). Note that row just worked is new RS row, as the collar will be turned down to reveal the RS of cast on edge.
Turn work and k2, p until 2 sts remain, k2.
Next row (RS): setup raglan shaping as follows: k6 (7, 7, 8, 9) kfb, k1, pm, kfb, k1, kfb, k1, pm, kfb, k13 (15, 15, 17, 19), kfb, k1, pm, kfb, k1, kfb, k1, pm, kfb, k7 (8, 8, 9, 10).
Next row (WS): k2, p until 2 sts remain (slipping all m as you come to them), k2.
Next row (RS): (k to 2 sts before m, kfb, k1, sl m, kfb) across (8 sts increased).
Rep last 2 rows until work measures 1.25 (1.25, 1.5, 1.75, 2.25)" from color change, ending on a WS row.
Next row (RS): work as established increasing at each m location, but at end of row do not turn. Pm and join to begin working in the round.
Knit one round even.
Next round: work increases as before: (k to 2 sts before m, kfb, k1, sl m, kfb) around.
Next round: knit.
Rep last 2 rounds until there are a total of 128 (132, 140, 152, 164) sts (work measures approximately 3 (3, 3.5, 3.75, 4)" from color change).
Knit even in the round until work

measures 4.25 (4.75, 5, 5.25, 5.5)" from color change, then divide for arms as follows: k to first raglan m, remove m, sl next 26 (24, 28, 30, 32) sts to scrap yarn or stitch holder, remove m, CO 2 sts for underarm, k across back sts to next m, remove m, sl next 26 (24, 28, 30, 32) sts to scrap yarn or stitch holder, remove m, CO 2 sts for underarm, k to end. Sleeve sts are now on hold and 80 (88, 88, 96, 104) sts rem on needles for body. Remove m for beginning of round, k 20 (22, 22, 24, 26) sts, replace m at underarm for new beginning of round. Knit even in the round until work measures 1 (1, 1, 2.25, 3.5)" from underarm.

Cut yarn, join CC1, and k 4 rounds even. Cut yarn, join MC, and k 1 round. Work rows 1–6 of Sweet Berries colorwork chart twice, then k 1 round even in MC. Cut yarns, join CC1 and knit one round even. Work in (k2, p2) rib in the round for 9 rounds, then BO loosely in pattern.

Sleeves
Return first set of held sts to double pointed needles, distributing sts evenly around 4 needles and using the fifth to knit. Join MC and pick up 1 stitch at left side of underarm gap, k around all sts, then pick up 1 stitch at right side of underarm gap. Pm and join to begin knitting in the round.
Knit even for 1 inch, then decrease 0 (2, 2, 0, 2) sts as follows: k1, k2tog, k around until 3 sts remain, ssk, k1. Work even until sleeve measures 3.75 (4.25, 5, 5.5, 6)" from underarm and cut yarn.
Join CC1 and k 1 round even. Work in (k2, p2) rib in the round for 9 rounds, then BO loosely in pattern. Rep all steps for second sleeve. Weave in all ends and block to finished measurements, folding down collar as you do so.

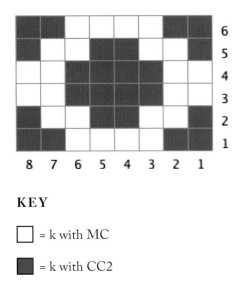

KEY

□ = k with MC

■ = k with CC2

TWO HANDED STRANDED COLORWORK

1: Keeping both yarns tensioned and ready to work, spread out the stitches on the right hand needle as you prepare to change colors.

2: Insert the right hand needle into the next stitch to be knit, using the middle finger (or whichever is most comfortable) to apply pressure to the backs of the stitches on the right hand needle to prevent them from sliding together.

3: The distance between color changes should never be more than 1 inch (4–5 sts in our gauge), as longer floats are more likely to snag with wearing.

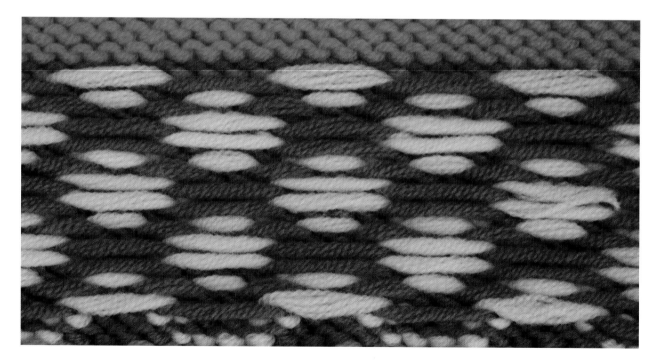

4: The wrong side of the work reveals the "floats" created by strands of unused colors. Consistently arranging the yarns so that the background color is in the right hand and the foreground, "pattern" color is in the left hand will result in a tidy wrong side.

Acknowledgements

Baby & Me Knits is truly a celebration of my family and friends. Thank you so much to my husband and co-photographer John for his inspiration, advice, and support. Thank you to my sweet son Jack – may you always look back on your infant modeling days with fondness and good humor! We love you to the moon and back. Thank you to my sister Hannah and to all of my friends and their children for modeling my knits – Lark and Boden, Alisa and Hailey, and Mandie and Penny. I hope you love the results! Thank you to my tireless parents, friends, and test knitters: Ava Scott, Alan Young, Jen Heinlein, Deb Reilly, Gretchen Mashmann, and Laura Ross. Your insight and suggestions were invaluable. Finally, thank you to my grandmothers Mary Young and Judith Scott for their faith in me, and to my great granny Viola, who would be completely thrilled to see my name in print.

Special thanks to Jo Bryant of BlueRed Press for her kindness and encouragement, Ashley Eipp for her gorgeous cover photography, Shannon Dunbabin of Cascade Yarns for her support, and Sandy Powers of Cape Cod Crochet for setting this adventure in motion.